DISHLICKERS

A MUSICAL
BY
DORIAN MODE

MUSIC, LYRICS, BOOK,
ORCHESTRATIONS

DORIAN MODE

FOR ALL ENQUIRIES CONTACT: ORiGiN™ Theatrical
PO BOX Q1235, QVB Post Office, Sydney, NSW, 1230, Australia
Phone: (61 2) 8514 5201 Fax: (61 2) 9299 2920
enquiries@originmusic.com.au   www.origintheatrical.com.au
Part of the ORiGiN™ Music Group
An Australian Independent Music Company

IMPORTANT NOTICE

should not be considered to be necessarily endorsing or otherwise attempting to promote an affiliation with any of the owners of the brand names or trademarks or public figures. Such references are solely for use in a dramatic context.

LANGUAGE NOTE

Licensees are welcome to make small alterations to the language that is used is this play so as to make it suitable for a younger cast and/or audience.

MUSIC USE NOTE

Licensees are solely responsible for obtaining formal written permission from copyright owners to use copyrighted music in the performance of this play and are strongly cautioned to do so. If no such permission is obtained by the licensee, then the licensee must use only original music that the licensee owns and controls. Licensees are solely responsible and liable for all music clearances and shall indemnify the copyright owners of the play(s) and their licensing agent, ORiGiN™ Theatrical, against any costs, expenses, losses and liabilities arising from the use of music by licensees. Please contact the appropriate music licensing authority in your territory for the rights to any incidental music. In Australia and New Zealand, contact APRA AMCOS apraamcos.com.au.

If you are in any doubt about any of the above then contact ORiGiN™ Theatrical.

For complete listing of plays and musicals available to perform and all licence enquiries, contact ORiGiN™ Theatrical.

---

www.origintheatrical.com.au
+ 61 2 8514 5201

4

AND HERE ARE THE RULES
IN PLAIN ENGLISH FOR YOU...

<u>DO NOT</u> perform this play without getting permission from ORiGiN™ Theatrical first. In 99% of cases you'll need to pay us money to be allowed to stage a performance. This money goes to the author(s) of the show who shed blood, sweat and tears creating this play. Please don't rob them of their livelihood.
Go online www.origintheatrical.com.au or call +61 2 8514 5201

<u>DO NOT</u> make a copy of this book by photocopying, scanning, taking a photo, retyping (on a computer or a typewriter), or using a pencil, pen or chalkboard. If you want to purchase more copies contact ORiGiN™ Theatrical.
Go online www.origintheatrical.com.au or call +61 2 8514 5201

<u>DO NOT</u> make any changes to the text without first getting permission from ORiGiN™ Theatrical in writing. Sometimes you'll be allowed to make changes and sometimes you won't. Please always check with us first.
Go online www.origintheatrical.com.au or call +61 2 8514 5201

<u>DO NOT</u> record your performances or rehearsals in anyway without first getting permission from ORiGiN™ Theatrical. We know everyone wants to try and record everything on their phones these days. We get it. But please don't encourage them or give them permission. Sometimes there are important contractual reasons as to why we can't give you permission to record it. And sometimes there aren't any reasons and we can say YES. Please just check with us first.
Go online www.origintheatrical.com.au or call +61 2 8514 5201

<u>DO</u> contact ORiGiN™ Theatrical if you have any questions about anything. At all. And we mean anything. One of us that works here (not me) has a peculiar interest in recording the unusual bird calls of the adult hoatzin (a species of tropical bird found in wet forest and mangrove of the Amazon and the Orinoco delta in South America) so we should be able to answer any questions you have about the Hoatzin. Plus we know some things about some other things too.

Thank you for taking the time to read this.

ALSO BY DORIAN MODE

Feedem Fighters

Millie's War

ABOUT THE AUTHOR

Dorian Mode M.A. (Hons) is the author of the comic novel, *A Café in Venice*, Penguin Books (Random House in Europe) and his comic memoir, *The Mozart Maulers*, also published by Penguin.

He has penned several short stories that have featured in bestselling Penguin anthologies such as *Girls Big Night Out 3* and *Heatwave, Penguin Summer Stories*.

He was a guest speaker at the Sydney Writer's Festival and read an abridged version of his second novel on ABC's Radio National (since repeated). His first novel was also released internationally as an audio book. In 2006 he was awarded a Varuna Literary Writing Fellowship and lectured in creative writing at Newcastle Uni.

His first and only screenplay was nominated for Best Unproduced Screenplay at the Australian Writer's Guild Awards and he was an IF Awards finalist again for Best Unproduced Screenplay the same year. (Best 'Never Produced' Screenplay, he often muses.)

He writes features for The Age and Sydney Morning Herald and was a weekend columnist for the Daily Telegraph under the pseudonym Beachcomber – a sitcom based on the column was optioned and made into a television pilot. He penned the back page column for Storyline, The Australian Writer's Guild Magazine and was also the back page columnist for Modern Fishing Magazine – the best selling fishing magazine in Australia. He is currently a regular travel feature writer for NRMA's Open Road Magazine.

His first play was produced in Sydney in 2011 with excellent reviews.

He has completed his doctorate in 2012 (APA scholarship) and lives on the NSW Central Coast with his wife and two children. He enjoys his local fishing club, pubs and playing snooker with anyone born between 24th of July and 23rd of August.

CHARACTERS
(In order of appearance)

LORRY   50+, blue singlet, flanno, shorts, work-
                   boots.

BEER BOTTLE   50+ high-viz aesthetic, shorts, thongs.

SHOWBAGS   50+ Moth-eaten Cronulla jersey,
                   trackies, thongs.

GRAHAM   early 30s, three-day-growth, collar, dog
                   suit.

GARY   late 20s, vet with a mullet.

WARWICK   early 20s, tradie chic.

SANDY   50+, bottle-blond, ex-pig-shooting
                   chick mum.

FELICITY   20s, pretty, lithe, Greenpeace aesthetic

LOLITA   20s, pretty, prissy, pampered, one-pice
                   dog suit

LIONEL   60+ comb-over and cheap clothes,
                   grimy.

TYSON   20s, muscled, menacing, tattooed,
                   skinhead.

HALLSY   50+, shock-jock, voice only.

TABATHA	50+, funky clothes, middle-class, artsy.
CHARLIE	50+, Italian suit jacket, white thongs, gold chains.

SETTING: The action takes place at the dog racing track at Gosford Showground, The Harrigan family home, Felicity's student apartment or Wamberal Beach.

ACT I

SCENE 1

EXT. GOSFORD SHOWGROUND DOG TRACK - NIGHT

We see three men studying the form-guide at the track, whilst sucking on beers. LORRY HARRIGAN (late 50's, blue singlet, flanno, shorts, work-boots), BEER BOTTLE (50s, high-viz aesthetic) and SHOWBAGS (50s, Cronulla Sharks jersey, trackies, thongs).

SHOWBAGS
Bottle and I cleaned up on your pooch last week. Made three-hundred smackers. What's he running in tonight, Loz?

LORRY
You've missed him. He's just run. Yeah, I had a feeling in me waters he'd at least place.

BEER BOTTLE
Missed him? Bugger! Stayed in the pub, too long. But we were smashing it on the pokes. Three jackpots between us.

SHOWBAGS
Mate, that dog'a yours is the fastest thing I've seen on four legs on this track for a long, long time. He won by a country *mile*. Where is he, anyway?

LORRY
I'm waiting for the steward to bring him over. He gets a schmacko when he wins. What's yer pick of the puppies tonight, Showbags?

SHOWBAGS
Injet Robbie. Manny's Boy is good value, too at three to one.

BEER BOTTLE
Loz, ever thought about racing him for the big money? Bags and I were talking about it at the fishing club the other night.

LORRY
(shrugs)
Never really considered it. How'd you think he'd go?

SHOWBAGS
Mate, he'd shit it in. Wouldn't he, Bottle?

BEER BOTTLE
(nodding)
Yep. He'd shit it in, Loz. That pooch of yours is the Phar Lap of dishlickers, fair dinkum.

LORRY
Reckon??

BEER BOTTLE
Mate, forget bloody Gosford! You need to race him in the Big Smoke?

LORRY
Sydney? Wentworth Park?

BEER BOTTLE
Nah, Sandown, mate. Melbourne. That's where the big
coin is.

LORRY
Melbourne? Long way.

GRAHAM (30s, three-day-growth, collar, dressed in a
one-piece dog suit) enters the stage with a steward
holding him on a leash. Graham is wearing a cage-
muzzle.

The steward exits.

GRAHAM
How much did yer have on me this time, Loz?

LORRY
(winks)
A few quiet shillings, mate.

Lorry pats Graham on the head and gives him a treat.

SHOWBAGS
We had a few dollars on yer the other night, too. You
ran like the clappers, champion. Well done!

GRAHAM
(incredulous)
Of course. I'm a trained athlete.

Graham stretches his hamstrings like a prize-fighter.

LORRY
(to Graham)

The boys reckon we should step up to the Big Smoke, Graham. What do you reckon, Champ? We've only ever raced you at Gosford. How'd you think you'd go in the city? Could ya handle the pressure?

GRAHAM
(thinking)
Maybe. What sort of dollars would we be lookin' at?

BEER BOTTLE
Well, the Superdog series pays the big money.

Graham thinks some more.

SHOWBAGS
(to Lorry)
First prize is three-hundred and fifty thousand.

GRAHAM
(whistles)
That's a lot of Smackos.

SHOWBAGS
(nodding)
Hellva lot of smackers.

LORRY
No he means "Smackos". Graham loves Smackos.

GRAHAM
(soto voce)
I could *kill* for a Smacko.

SHOWBAGS
(To Lorry)

Loz, that puppie's a fair dinkum pocket-rocket. It's time to start thinkin' about movin' up to the city.

LORRY
Movin' up to the city??

BEER BOTTLE
Wanna be wasting him in the boon docks for the rest of yer life? Time to cash in, Loz.

LORRY
Do you really think he could go all the way?

SHOWBAGS
Loz, trust me. That little puppy'a yours could win Sandown running backwards.

Graham mimes running backwards, before busting into Michael Jackson type moon-dance moves.

LORRY
(thinking)
Maybe you're right...

Lorry nods, considers Graham and thinks.

LORRY (cont'd)
(sings)

"MOVIN' UP TO THE CITY"

I'M SITTIN' HERE IN'A GOSFORD PARK
PICKIN' ALL THE PUPPIES JUST AS SOON AS IT'S DARK
SICK'A PICKIN' PUPPIES FOR NO REAL REASON
HOPE I'M NOT HERE PICKIN' FOR ANOTHER

DAMN SEASON
GUESS I'M KILLIN' TIME
WITH NOTHIN' TO LOSE
PICKIN' ALL THE PUPPIES AND A SUCKIN' ON
BOOZE

I DON'T DIG THIS TRACK ONE BIT
HAD ENOUGH OF THIS COUNTRY SHIT!
I'M MOVIN UP TO THE CITY
(ENSEMBLE - INCLUDING GRAHAM) HE'S
MOVIN UP TO THE CITY

I'M SICK AND TIRED OF RUSTIC CHARM
SICK'A THE COUNTRY, SICK OF THE FARM
THE CITY'S MIGHT PRETTY WHILE YOUR
CHEWIN ON CUD
OR BREAKIN YOUR BUTT WITH A MUTT IN THE
MUD
SICK'A KILLIN TIME
FOREVER IT SEEMS
TIME TO DIP MY CUP INTO A BUCKET OF
DREAMS

I DON'T DIG THIS TRACK ONE BIT
HAD ENOUGH OF THIS COUNTRY SHIT!
I'M MOVIN UP TO THE CITY
(ENSEMBLE) HE'S MOVIN UP TO THE CITY

Instrumental break as the cast dance their hearts out.

I'M SICK AND TIRED OF RUSTIC CHARM
SICK'A THE COUNTRY, SICK OF THE FARM
THE CITY'S MIGHT PRETTY WHILE YOUR

CHEWIN ON CUD
OR BREAKIN YOUR BUTT WITH A MUTT IN THE
MUD
SICK'A KILLIN TIME
FOREVER IT SEEMS
TIME TO DIP MY CUP INTO A BUCKET OF
DREAMS

I DON'T DIG THIS TRACK ONE BIT
HAD ENOUGH OF THIS COUNTRY SHIT!
I'M MOVIN UP TO THE CITY
(ENSEMBLE) HE'S MOVIN UP TO THE CITY

The dog track breaks away as we...

TRANSITION TO:

INT. HARRIGAN FAMILY HOME GOSFORD -
LATER

The music continues softly on the piano as the stage is
transformed into a family home.

Lorry sits in his timeworn Jason Recliner in front of the
telly, which flashes in front of the cast, centre-stage - a
lighting effect.

We see greyhound paraphernalia all over the stage. A
sign reads A HOUSE IS NOT A HOME WITHOUT A
GREYHOUND.

Lorry's two sons enter and sit on the oversized 80s lounge watching TV with Lorry. GARY (late 20s, intelligent-looking) is reading a text book and WARWICK (early 20s, high-viz) is reading a tabloid newspaper.

LORRY
Good to see the rain has finally stopped, luv.

SANDY (O.S.)
You know what that means but.

LORRY
(to Sandy offstage)
No what?

SANDY (O.S.)
Slugs.

LORRY
(to the boys, nodding)
Slugs.

SANDY (O.S.)
Me garden will be full of slugs. You watch.

SANDY HARRIGAN (50s, bottle blond, aging pig-shooting chick aesthetic) enters with Lorry's dinner on a tray. It looks bland, indeed.

LORRY
Now, what *masterpiece* have you made us tonight, luv?

SANDY
(proudly)

Pork Chops Italiano. Andy shot the feral himself. So it's fresh.

LORRY
Yum-o!

Graham, sits in a chair, reading the form-guide while drinking a glass of blue water with a cocktail umbrella in it.

GRAHAM
(reading form guide, drinking)
Save the bones for me, boys.

Lorry notices the drink.

LORRY
Graham, you haven't been drinking from the toilet, again, have you mate?

GRAHAM
(looking guilty)
Why...why do you ask?

LORRY
Mate, that blue water's not safe for dogs to drink. You know that, right?

GRAHAM
(looking at glass)
You mean it's not an energy drink?

SANDY
Energy drink?? It's to disguise the toilet water.

WARWICK

In other words: to hide our shit.

SANDY
Language.

GRAHAM
What is it with you people and hiding your shit? Shit is
a beautiful thing. Liberate the turd, I say!

SANDY
Language, Graham.

GRAHAM
Sorry, Sandy. (to boys) Hey, I see here Barney's Little
Helper placed at Dapto. I'm surprised. He's really let
himself go, that bloke. Ever since the family got Netflix.

WARWICK
(from corner of his mouth)
He's on the gear.

GRAHAM
Really?

WARWICK
They all are. That's why you can never win the big ones.
Like at Wentworth Park.

LORRY
(thinking, worried)
Reckon?

WARWICK
Course.

GARY

(emphatically)
Not true. We're testing all the time.

LORRY
Really?

Sandy returns with her own meal on a tray and sits.

GARY
"Trust me I'm a doctor."

WARWICK
You're a bloody vet.

GARY
(angrily)
Same thing.

LORRY
My boy "the doctor", eh? Dr Harrigan. Who would'a
thought it?

SANDY
(indicating Warwick)
Not that there's anything wrong with being a gyprocker.
Isn't that right, Father?

LORRY
(catching on)
Oh oh yes yes, of course, luv Hey, look at me. I'm a
truck driver and the happiest bloke in Gosford.

SANDY
And I'm a professional dog groomer. And no one's
happier than me.

LORRY
Celebrity dog groomer.

SANDY
Ha ha. True. That Julie from *Masterchef* has the nicest
French poodle.

GRAHAM
Is she single?

The Graham pulls out a pocket mirror and checks his
face.

SANDY
I'll ask.

GRAHAM
French poodle, eh? Does she have an accent?

LORRY
(stands)
Okay family. I'd like to make a special announcement.
(clears his throat) I've made an important decision
today. And I spose it affects all of ewes.

WARWICK
We're going paint-balling!

LORRY
No.

GARY
We are buying a bigger tinnie!

LORRY
No no. We might but. If it all works out.

SANDY
What's is it, luv?

LORRY
(excitedly)
We're racing Graham in Melbourne for the *Super Dog
Series*!

SANDY
Have you been talking to those two pelicans, Showbags
and Beer Bottle, again?

LORRY
So?

SANDY
So?? *So*??? One win at Gosford and they think
Graham's Phar Lap.

GRAHAM
(aside)
I *am* fast. But I thought it was the energy drinks.

LORRY
He *is* fast.

SANDY
Lorry, we don't have the capital or the cattle to race for
big money.

GRAHAM
(aside)
Cattle? Is that an oblique reference to me?

SANDY

We don't even have the coin to get the bloody tinnie's outboard fixed, luv.

GARY

Mum's right, Dad. It's thousands of dollars in accommodation, special flights, kennels. A couple of my clients race interstate. It's a whole other ball game. And is Graham really up for it? He might run okay at Gosford but the whole thing could be a waste of good money.

GRAHAM

(angrily)

I *am* in the room.

WARWICK

One thing I know. He's the fastest greyhound we've *ever* bred. Isn't that right, Dad?

LORRY

Sure is, son.

GRAHAM

(confused)

So you're definitely saying it's *not* the energy drinks?

WARWICK

Graham, it's dunny water!

GRAHAM

(thinking, soto voce)

So I *am* really fast?

LORRY

Should'a seen him fly at Gosford last night. Could have run the last 100 metres backwards.

Graham starts jogging around the stage - behind the furniture etc backwards.

SANDY
(to Warwick)
Lorry, we can't afford to service the gearbox for the truck and you-

LORRY
Listen luv, I've dreamed of this all me life. Just never had the cattle.

GRAHAM
(aside)
I think it's clear I'm the "cattle".

Suddenly, we hear a mobile ring (O.S). The ringtone is the sound of a dog barking. Lorry fishes in his pocket.

LORRY
Hellooo...? G'day Showbags! *Maaate*, I was just tellin the family about the Super Dog Series at Sandown and...the...the...ABC? (stands up - moves towards the telly) Mate, I don't even know if this TV gets the ABC. Is that channel 2? What? *Four Corners*? What's that, mate? Is that like *The Block*? Current Affairs...?

SANDY
No that's Channel Nine, *Current Affair*. (to the boys) I never miss it. It's good to be across important issues. Last night was all about buying the right bra. You'd be surprised how many women are wearing the wrong bra for their cup-size.

WARWICK
(To Gary, winking)

Yeah, it was great television! More boobs than *Game of Thrones*.

SANDY
Language! Now, take me for instance. I'm normally a C-cup but since having kids I-

LORRY
(to Gary)
Gary, do we have the ABC on this telly?

GARY
(stands)
Let me check.

WARWICK
That's that government station. Remember, we watched it once with those bush fires. Black Wednesday. Or was it Black Thursday?

SANDY
Red Friday.

The stage-lights dim and the orchestra plays a SOUR MELODY.

We see the family in the flickering light of the TV, open-mouthed.

Graham drops his chew.

Sandy leads Graham offstage, hiding his face from the TV.

Lights up.

Lorry jumps up from his big chair.

LORRY
Those stupid *pricks*!

SANDY (O.S.)
Language, father!

LORRY
Don't you see what those live-baiters have done, Sandy?
Now we're all tarred with the same brush!

SANDY
Ahh, it'll blow over. It's one rogue element. It's not like
they can shut down an entire industry.

GARY
Mum's right, Dad. It'll blow over. Forget about it.

WARWICK
Blow over? *Blow over*??! We won't be able to walk
Graham down the street without people thinking we're
live-baiters and dog killers.

SANDY
City people! They should see me brother Andy hunting
feral pigs? Gary's right. It'll blow over.

LORRY
(incensed)
Were you watching the same program? This will have a
ripple effect through the entire industry. Be honest.
What were you *really* thinking watching that, Sandy?

SANDY

Truly? I was thinking that that snotty-nosed presenter wasn't a *patch* on Tracey Grimshaw. (to Gary) Tracey's lost weight again, too. (winks) Jenny Craig. Big feature in *New Idea* about it.

GARY
You were on Jenny Craig for a while, Mum, weren't you?

SANDY
Lost five kilos.

WARWICK
Why'd you stop?

LORRY
(exacerbated)
Now we're talking about diets!

SANDY
Well, that's what I expect from a decent current affairs show, Lorry. I'm interested in diets. Diets and bras. Okay?

Warwick jumps fto his feet.

WARWICK
(slapping his head)
Dad, I just remembered!

LORRY
What son?

WARWICK
It's the ABC.

GARY
So?

WARWICK
The A-B-C!!

LORRY
What's your point, son?

WARWICK
Hellooo?? Who watches the ABC?

They all come to the same realisation one by one before
detonating with laughter, relieved.

LORRY
(epiphany)
Of course! It's just those bloody culture vultures that
watch the ABC.

SANDY
Aside from Landline, no one watches the ABC in the
bush, I'll tell ya that right now.

LORRY
True. Alan Jones and Hallsy say the ABC represents 1%
of the population.

SANDY
(winks)
No red-blooded pig shootin' bush gal would be caught
dead watchin the ABC.

LORRY
Geeze, that takes me back. That's were we first met. Pig
shootin' in Dunedoo. Remember?

SANDY
It was romantic.

LORRY
Yer Mum was a top sort then, too, boys.

WARWICK
Ahh, too much information.

LORRY
Cover girl.

WARWICK/GARY
Cover girl??

LORRY
(opening magazine)
Yep still got the magazine somewhere. Now where did I
put it? Was only looking at it the other day. Ah, here it
is. *Bacon Busters*. The centrefold section. *Bores and
Babes*. Your Mum was *Miss November*. Had it enlarged
as a poster in me garage at the time. Had it laminated.

Lorry shows the boys (and audience) a poster of a
bikini-clad woman cradling a rifle, straddling a dead
feral pig.

GARY
Wow! You never told us that, Mum!

LORRY
She was a crack shot with a twenty-two, your Mum.

SANDY
(arching an eyebrow)
Was?

LORRY
(winks)
Still are. She was a wild hard drinking bush gal when I
met her. But I've tamed her somewhat.

Sandy offers Lorry a wry, coquettish smile.

LORRY (cont'd)
(sings)

"SANDY"

SANDY
MY EVER-FERAL SANDY
SHE IS ROUGH BUT HANDY
WITH A .22
I THINK THAT GIRL SHE UNDERSTANDS ME
MY VODKA-SCULLING SANDY
AND SANDY COMES IN HANDY
WHEN YOU'RE IN A BLUE

SANDY
HER MODUS OPERANDI
IS TO SCULL A BRANDY
AND A VODKA CHASER, TOO
BUT WHEN I STOP THE UTE IT'S HANDY
FOR MY VODKA-SCULLING SANDY
CAUSE SANDY'S NONE TO DANDY
WHEN SHE HAS TO SPEW

SHE LIKES PIG SHOOTING AND
STRONG HOME BREW
SCULLING CONTESTS
AND POPPING ROOS
SHE HATES LEFTIES

SHE HATES GREENIES
SHE LIKES GUNS AND HIGH BIKINIS

OH SANDY
MY EVER FERAL SANDY
AND HER BROTHER ANDY
HE'S A FERAL TOO
HE LIKES TO VENT HIS RAGES
BY FIGHTING BLOKES IN CAGES
WHILE SANDY OFTEN WAGES
A LAZY DOLLAR TOO

(INSTRUMENTAL BREAK)

SHE'S NOT ONE FOR SOCIAL GRACES
LIKES TO BURP IN PUBLIC PLACES
LIFTS HER LEG TO FART IN CHURCHES
AT MELBOURNE CUP
SHE'S DRUNK AND LURCHES

SANDY
MY EVER-FERAL SANDY
VODKA MAKES HER RANDY
SO I NEED TO GET HER HOME
SHE COOKS A GOURMET MEAL, MY SANDY
CHOPS 'ITALIANDI'
WITH TOMATOES FROM A CAN
DEMAND TO BE IN ROME

SHE'S MY EVER FERAL GAL FROM DUNEDOO
AND BEFORE SHE PASSES OUT
SHE'S FUNNY TOO
OH SANDY
OH SANDY MINE
SHE'S MY EVER FERAL GAL FROM DUNEDOO

AND WHEN SHE SHOOTS PIG
SHE EATS IT TOO
OH SANDY
SANDY MINE

The lights fade on stage right as we bring up lights on stage left and ...

TRANSITION TO:

INT. FELICITY BLISS'S FLAT GOSFORD - EVENING

We see a modest student flat. The decor can best be described as 'early milk-crate'. We see peTA signs and animal rights paraphernalia over the set. And shelves and shelves of books.

FELICITY (20s, computer tan, Greenpeace aesthetic) reads Dostoevsky with the sound down on the TV.

LOLITA (20s, prissy, dressed in one-pice dog suit) sits at her feet while also reading, Dostoevsky.

We hear WHALE VOCALISATIONS as Felicity's mobile rings.

FELICITY
(answering phone)
Hello Terry. Oh, nothing. Just reading. What? What?? *Four Corners*? I'll switch it over now. God, who watches commercial television? It's ABC or SBS or nothing...

We hear the same sour melody we hear from the previous scene.

As the TV flickers, Lolita cries, comforted by Felicity.

TRANSITION TO:

EXT. GOSFORD SHOWGROUND - NIGHT

It's dog racing night at Gosford Showground. Any and all extras are on stage looking like busy punters.

We hear an ANNOUNCER CALL A RACE.

Lorry, Showbags, Bottle and Graham enter the stage. Graham is wearing a cage-muzzle.

BEER BOTTLE
Good to see the rain has finally stopped.

LORRY
You know what that means but.

SHOWBAGS
What?

LORRY
Slugs.

They all nod, pensively.

SHOWBAGS
Mate, did you hear. Since *Four Corners*, Baird is launching an inquiry into the industry.

LORRY
Mate, those live baiters have really let us all down. That
bloody Lionel is one of them.

SHOWBAGS
(pointing)
Yeah, saw him earlier. He's racing Tyson in the 4th. I'm
told (lowers his voice) for the right "price", he'll make
your dog disappear.

GRAHAM
(alarmed)
What does that mean? Disappear??

BEER BOTTLE
(winks)
You know, The Big Sleep.

GRAHAM
Isn't that a movie with Humphrey Bogart?

LORRY
How do you know that?

GRAHAM
Sandy watches a lot of daytime television.

BEER BOTTLE
Look out here he comes!

LIONEL (60s) comb-over and cheap clothes, walks
over. With him is TYSON, (20s, angry tattooed
skinhead) He too has a muzzle-cage. Tyson sneers at
Graham. Graham sneers back.

LORRY

G'day Lionel. Did you hear there's going to be an enquiry after that *Four Corners* turnout?

LIONEL
Bloody Greenies! They're gunner ruin it for *everyone*.

LORRY
(looking askance at the boys)
Only for live baiters and dog killers.

The boys nod.

LIONEL
Mate, face facts. Live-baiting is all about the winning edge.

LORRY
Dog racing is all about getting together with yer sons an' that and (nodding at Showbags and Bottle) yer mates. Its about family.

LIONEL
Family? What *are* you smoking, Harrigan? It's about *money*. It always has been. And always will be. Gambling is the bedrock of the sport.

LORRY
(heatedly)
It's about being part of a community of like-minded people. Greyhound people.

LIONEL
Well, a little birdy tells me you're running that mangy mutt'a yours at Sandown, this year?

LORRY

So?

Lionel laughs out loud.

LIONEL
You don't think that flea-bag of yours is gunner win the
Super Dog Series without live-baiting do you? You
gotta blood 'im, Harrigan.

GRAHAM
(aside)
Is he referring to me? Fleas? Sandy has a dog grooming
business. I'm one of the best smelling greyhounds this
side of-

LORRY
Listen, Lionel! My father raced dogs. And *his* father
before him. We did it clean. Without doping, live
baiting, or killing dud dogs. It's people like you, Lionel,
that have dragged our sport into the gutter! The public
despise us, thanks to people like you.

Lionel gets in Lorry's face.

LIONEL
Yeah, well when you want to compete at Sandown.
When you want your dog to have the winning edge,
come and see me. They all do in the end - sooner or
later.

Lionel sings, with Tyson joining in with a harmony on
the bridge.
"BAIT SONG"

RABBITS AND POSSUMS
AND KILL EM AND TOSS EM

AND POP EM INTO THE BIN
TIE EM TO A STICK
THAT'LL DO THE TRICK
BETTER BACK IT QUICKER THAN OLD GUNSIN

POSSUMS AND PIGLETS
LET'S SHAKE IT AND JIGGLE IT
AND SEND IT AROUND AGAIN
LOOK IT IN THE EYE
LET IT SLOWLY DIE
LET THOSE DOGGIES FLY AROUND THE TRACK
AGAIN

AND IF YOUR POOCH
IS RUNNING LIKE A MOOCH
AND THEN YOU NEVER FIND HIM OUT OF BED
JUST COME WITH ME
I'LL TIE HIM TO A TREE
AND THEN I'LL PUT A BULLET IN HIS HEAD!

KITTENS AND CHICKENS
AND BUDGIES THAT SICKENS
AND GUINEA PIGS QUICKEN YOUR HOUND
GOTTA KEEP IT REAL
GOTTA HEAR IT SQUEAL
GOTTA GET A LITTLE BLOOD IN THAT SOUND

(INSTRUMENTAL BREAK - LIONEL AND TYSON
DANCE)

AND IF YOUR MUTT
IS RUNNING WITH A GUT
AND NOW HE'S GOT A LITTLE MIDDLE AGE
SPREAD
COME WITH ME

I'LL TAKE HIM TO THE SEA
AND THEN I'LL STUFF HIM IN A SACK WITH
LEAD!

BOXES OF FOXES
AND WOMBATS AND SUGAR BATS
WATER RATS ARE RENOWNED
GOTTA KEEP IT REAL
GOTTA HEAR IT SQUEAL
GOTTA KEEP GOTTA KEEP EM MEAN
GOTTA LET IT SCREAM
GOTTA KEEP GOTTA KEEP IT REAL
GOTTA HEAR IT SQUEAL
GOTTA GET A LITTLE BLOOD IN THAT SOUND

The backstage fades to black as we...

TRANSITION TO:

EXT. WAMBERAL BEACH - DAY

We hear a SEASCAPE as Warwick walks along the
beachfront stage.

WARWICK
(to Graham O.S.)
Graham, just clam down, mate. I know you're excited.
But remember, *don't* drink the sea water. You know
what happens!

Graham enters stage-right with a dead bird in his mouth.
He drops it at Warwick's feet.

GRAHAM

What do you mean don't drink the sea water?

WARWICK
Remember what happened last time. Seawater goes
straight through you, mate. The car stunk like Satan's
arsehole for a week.

GRAHAM
I thought it was Sandy's leftover Burrito that went
through me.

WARWICK
No, it was from drinking seawater, mate.

Felicity and Lolita enter stage-left.

Warwick immediately sniffs Lolita's rear end. Lolita is
slightly flattered but annoyed.

WARWICK (cont'd)
Graham, stop doing that. Sorry. He gets excited at the
beach.

GRAHAM
(sniffing, aside)
I just love arseholes.

LOLITA
(to Warwick)
It's a dog thing. Don't worry about it.

GRAHAM
Hi, I'm Graham but my stage name is *Kinky Boots*. I'm a
legend in racing circles. You may have heard about me.
Tell me about yourself. What star-sign are you, darling?

Warwick throws a tennis-ball into the wings.

GRAHAM (cont'd)
Balls!!!

Graham tears off-stage after it.

Lolita causally follows.

Felicity and Warwick chat but are both distracted by their manic greyhounds. They look beyond the audience - into the imaginary distance without looking at each other

FELICITY
(looking ahead)
  Hi, I'm Felicity. And that's my greyhound, Lolita.

WARWICK
(looking ahead)
  I'm Warwick. (points) That idiot drinking seawater over there is, Graham.

FELICITY
They love the beach, don't they? I love seeing them run free. Free as nature intended.

WARWICK
Yeah it's Graham's favourite thing in the world - aside from turds. Wamby is great for dogs, isn't it? Only beach on the Coast they can run free. So what got you into greyhounds?

FELICITY
She's a rescue dog.

WARWICK
(distracted)
Graham don't drink the seawater!

GRAHAM (O.S.)
But I'm *thirsty*, Warwick!

FELICITY
I work for peTA.

WARWICK
Peter? I worked for Peter for years. I saw Peter at the track on Chewsdee night?

FELICITY
Yes. And we'll all be there for the next meeting. Will be huge, I reckon. Since *Four Corners*.

WARWICK
Yeah, should be a big night. We all need to stand together.

FELICITY
I agree. Lolita, come away from that dead seagull.

LOLITA (O.S.)
It might be still alive. Shall we call WIRES?

WARWICK
How long have you worked for Peter?

FELICITY
Lolita! Leave that bird alone! We can't help it now. Sorry what did you say?

WARWICK

Have you worked for Peter, long?

GRAHAM (O.S.)
Is just a *little* seawater okay, Woz? Like maybe a midi's worth?

WARWICK
No!

FELICITY
Just part time. I'm studying English Lit at Ourimbah campus. What do you do?

WARWICK
Gyprocker. Graham! Leave that dead bird alone!

FELICITY
Hip Rocker? Do you do that full-time? What's your day job?

WARWICK
What? Um yeah. That *is* my day job. But my life is all about the dogs, of course.

FELICITY
Me too.

They both turn to each other.

A moment.

FELICITY (cont'd)
(coquettishly)
Well, I better head back. When I'm not at uni or studying, PeTA demands most of my time.

WARWICK
Yeah Peter's like that. I remember.

FELICITY
Have you worked for PeTA, too?

WARWICK
For years. After school. Mostly cleaning out kennels.

FELICITY
Been there done that. Well, I hope we meet down here
again, Warwick. Or maybe I'll see you at the next dog
race at Gosford.

WARWICK
Wouldn't miss it. The whole family'll be there.

FELICITY
Really? Wow! Okay, hope to meet again.

They shake hands.

Felicity and Lolita exit.

Warwick and Graham are love-struck and open-
mouthed.

GRAHAM
I feel funny in the tummy, Warwick.

WARWICK
Me too, mate.

GRAHAM
What just happened?

WARWICK
Love.

GRAHAM
Love?

WARWICK
(sings)

Warwick sings - with Graham steeling lines and
harmonising.

"LOVE FELL FROM THE SKY"

LOVE, FELL RIGHT FROM THE SKY
STRAIGHT FROM HEAVEN ABOVE
RIGHT SMACK IN THE EYE
IN A MOMENT
IN A FEELING
IN THE BLINK OF AN EYE
MY STUNNED HEART'S REELING
HOW MY HEART FINDS THIS MADNESS SO
APPEALING
SWEET AS HONEY
AND KIND OF HEALING

LOVE, BUMPED INTO MY HEART
IT LANDED A PUNCH
THAT CRACKED FROM THE START
IS THIS LOVE?
IS THIS LOVE?
THIS FEELING
(TOGETHER) FROM HEAVEN ABOVE

(INSTRUMENTAL BREAK)

HOW MY HEART FINDS THIS MADNESS SO
APPEALING
SWEET AS HONEY
AND KIND OF HEALING

LOVE, BUMPED INTO MY HEART
IT LANDED A PUNCH
THAT CRACKED FROM THE START
IS THIS LOVE?
IS THIS LOVE?
(TOGETHER) THIS FEELING
FROM HEAVEN ABOVE

GRAHAM
I feel funny in the tummy, Warwick.

WARWICK
That's love at first sight, Graham.

GRAHAM
No, I mean I feel funny in the tummy. It's Sandy's
Burrito all over again.

WARWICK
(furious)
I told you not to drink the seawater, Graham!

Blackout.

We hear a protracted giant WET FART in the darkness.

TRANSITION TO:

INT. FELICITY BLISS'S FLAT GOSFORD - DAY

Sandy is blow-drying Lolita in a bathtub mid-stage.

Felicity enters.

FELICITY
You'll be the best smelling dog on the Central Coast, little missy. It's great you can come to the customers. So convenient.

SANDY
Yeah. It's all in me trailer. It's a franchise. They give it to yer when you buy the business, an that.

FELICITY
(smelling Lolita)
This new conditioner smells lovely.

SANDY
Yeah, the company make it up special. Not the usual crap you buy from the pet shop.

FELICITY
How much do I owe you?

SANDY
You're a student, right?

FELICITY
Yes. But I work part time for peTA.

SANDY
Peter?

FELICITY

PeTA. People for the Ethical Treatment of Animals. Lolita's a rescue dog.

Felicity looks at Sandy's Greyhound T-shirt.

FELICITY (cont'd)
Lolita's a rescue dog. I see you're into greyhounds, too. You must really-

SANDY
Racing them, sure.

There's an awkward moment.

FELICITY
That's where we disagree, I'm afraid.

SANDY
I've seen your lot at the track. Protesting, an that. Making a fuss.

FELICITY
Making a *fuss*? Well, it shouldn't take the ABC to highlight cruel and abhorrent practices in the dog racing industry. The country's appalled, frankly.

SANDY
Yes, the footage *was* appalling. I'll admit that. But why do ewes have to tar us all with the same brush? Me hubby and me aren't live-baiting or killing dud dogs. We love these animals as much as ewes do. Your mob don't have a monopoly on loving pets, you know. Dogs are me life.

FELICITY

Well, there's some common ground, at least. What do I owe you?

SANDY
Students $25. People form peTA pay $30.

An awkward silence.

FELICITY
(handing over $30)
Ten, twenty, thirty. I'll see you at the next race meeting.

SANDY
Not if I see yer first.

Felicity and Lolita exit the stage in high dudgeon.

Sandy surreptitiously gives them the finger.

TRANSITION TO:

EXT. GOSFORD SHOWGROUND RACE TRACK - NIGHT

Lorry, Showbags and Beer Bottle pick dogs on the form guide while sucking on beers. Graham sits cross-legged reading a novel in his muzzle.

BEER BOTTLE
(to Graham)
Whatcha reading, Graham?

GRAHAM

Nabokov. This new greyhound I'm seeing at the beach is really into Russian writers. [thinks] Russian writers are quite dark, aren't they?

SHOWBAGS
I'm reading a dark book at the moment.

LORRY
What's that?

SHOWBAGS
Fifty Shades Darker.

BEER BOTTLE
Is that better than the movie?

SHOWBAGS
Nah. But it's awkward getting a boner on the building site. Makes Fitzy quite uncomfortable when we're scaffolding. He reckons it's sexual harassment.

GRAHAM
(reading, without looking up)
Yeah, I hate it when the old lipstick comes out. At least you blokes have trousers.

LORRY
50 Shades, eh? I'll tell young Warwick to read it.

SHOWBAGS
That's right. He's got a new bird. How's that going for him?

LORRY
Well, I wouldn't say "new bird" exactly. He's been meeting this girl down at the beach. She's into

greyhounds and that but a bit of a culture vulture, he reckons. Never met a girl quite like her. Bit different. High brow.

SHOWBAGS
(dreamily)
Young love, hey?

BEER BOTTLE
(dreamily)
Young bloody love.

LORRY
Mate, how long's it been since you had a lady friend in yer life, Showbags?

BEER BOTTLE
Loz, the last time "Bags" was inside a woman was when he visited the Statue of Liberty.

SHOWBAGS
Piss off. (thinking) I spose the last date I had was that terrible date back in me home town, Cronulla.

BEER BOTTLE
That's right. The famous "Shelia from the Shire". That date was the day of the Cronulla Riot, wasn't it?

SHOWBAGS
Yep. Talk about timing, geeze. How was I to know the joint would go ballistic and I'd end up with free curry for a year?

LORRY
Free *curry*??

BEER BOTTLE
(laughing)
Yeah, he saved some poor Indian bloke from the mob.
Little fella was so grateful he gave Bags a year's worth
of free curry at his restaurant. And Bags *hates* curry
(laughs).

SHOWBAGS
(to Lorry)
Yeah. Poor little bloke had nuthun to do with nuthun.
He was just out with his family for the day. They were
gunner bash his brains out. Dickheads. I had to chin
some tattooed Nazi before taking this poor Indian bloke
to the hospital. By then me date disappeared into the
crowd.

BEER BOTTLE
Did you ever here from her, again?

SHOWBAGS
Nup. It was such a bad first-date she never retuned me
calls. Can you blame her? (chuckles sadly) Surreal day.
Mad. As the day wore on things got worse. By evening
the town was in lock-down. Cars on fire. Shops
smashed. I kept telling me date it would all blow over.
Trying to keep the romance going, type of thing, you
know... Cause I really liked this bird. I *really* did. She
was *magic*.

LORRY
You've never told me the whole story, mate. What
happened exactly?

SHOWBAGS
(sings- with Bottle)

I was in love with her since school. Never had the courage to ask her out. She was outta my league kinda thing. Use to fantasise about her all the time. I was smitten...

"MOONLIGHT IN THE SHIRE"

SB: OH, HOW I YEARNED FOR JUST ONE NIGHT
BB: A BOOZY RENDEZVOUS TO WOO HER
SB: HOW I LEARNED OLD MURPHY'S RIGHT.
BB: YOU DO BELIEVE IN HOODOO, DO YOU?
SB: I PICKED A LAZY MOONLIT SUNDAY
BB: TO ASK HER ON A DATE
SB: I HAD TO PICK THAT CRAZY ONE DAY
BB: OH, THE FICKLE HAND OF FATE
SB: OH YES THE WHOLE JOINT WENT BERSERK
LH: ROMANCE WOULDN'T WORK?
SB: (NUP) I WON'T DENY IT, IT WAS
SB,BB: QUITE A RIOT!

(SHOWBAGS SINGS, EYES GLAZED IN MEMORY)

WALKING HAND IN HAND
I JUST IGNORE THE MOB THAT'S PASSING
I DON'T SEE THE SHARKIES FAN
OR SEE THE MAN HE'S GLASSING
'TWAS HER CAPTIVATING EYES
THAT SET MY SOUL ON FIRE
SB,BB,LH: MOONLIGHT IN THE SHIRE

I IGNORE THE CHANTING MOB
THE SCREECHING TATTOOED BIMBO
OR MUSIC FROM A TELEVISION

HURLED THROUGH A SHOP-FRONT WINDOW
'TWAS HER GENTLE SOOTHING VOICE
THAT WAS HEAVEN'S SWEETEST CHOIR
SB,BB,LH: MOONLIGHT IN THE SHIRE

WE WALKED ALONG THE MOONLIT SHORE
WHERE DOZY COPS DID HUDDLE
TO TIPTOE THROUGH THE BROKEN GLASS
FOR A COSY SPOT TO CUDDLE

HER SWEET PERFUME IDEALLY WINS
THE SMELL OF BURNING WHEELIE BINS
HER EYES WERE GLAZED WITH TEARS THAT
DAY
BUT WAS IT LOVE, OR PEPPER SPRAY?
I'D TAKE HER FAR AWAY
BUT SOMEONE SLASHED MY TYRE
SB,BB,LH: MOONLIGHT IN THE SHIRE

(INSTRUMENTAL BREAK - THE BOYS
ROMANTICALLY DANCE WITH EACH OTHER -
HAMMING IT UP)

I TRIED TO WOO HER ALL I COULD
MY REPARTEE WAS CHARMING
BUT SITTING WITH A CUPPA TEA
THE TEARGAS WAS ALARMING

WHILE HARD FOR HER TO COMPREHEND
I DIDN'T WANT THE DAY TO END
BUT IT WASN'T IN MY WACKY PLAN
TO HIDE A MAN FROM PAKISTAN
OH HER PRETTY FACE AGLOW
BESIDE A CAR ON FIRE
SB,BB,LH: MOONLIGHT IN THE SHIRE

INT. HARRIGAN FAMILY HOME GOSFORD - DAY

Sandy is ironing when Lorry storms in holding the
Daily Telegraph aloft.

LORRY
The world has ended as we know it!!

SANDY
What on earth-

LORRY
Baird is shutting down the *entire* dog racing industry in
NSW. All over red rover.

SANDY
What?? He can't do that!

LORRY
In the words of Tony Abbott, he's made a "captain's
call".

SANDY
Bloody captain's calls! I'm jack of them. Are we living
in a democracy or a dictatorship?

Graham enters chewing a giant lamb bone.

GRAHAM
What's going on?

SANDY
They're shutting down the dog racing industry. It's all
over.

LORRY
Finito.

GRAHAM
(shocked)
So I can't compete anymore?

LORRY
That's it. Our life as we know it is finished.

SANDY
Don't be melodramatic. We'll do something else.

GRAHAM
But athletics is me whole life?

LORRY
Not no more, mate. You'll just have to read more
Russian books.

GRAHAM
This is *unbelievable*. I'm telling the sausage dog twins
next door.

Graham exits the stage. We hear DOGS BARKING
O.S.

The barking suddenly stops.

GRAHAM (O.S.) (cont'd)
Mate, it can't be Sergio. He had his nuts whipped of by
our Gary three years ago.

We hear barking O.S.

GRAHAM (O.S.) (cont'd)

No. Dog years. And another thing. The blue water's *not* an energy drink, after all.

LORRY
What am I gunner do, Sandy? Dog racing is me life. I got nuthun else.

SANDY
It's not your entire life. There's more to Lorry Harrigan than dog racing and getting on the turps every Chewsdee night with those melons, Showbags and Beer Bottle. Look at Graham. Since meeting that dog down at the beach he's getting into Russian literature.

LORRY
Russian *literature*? Have you been breathing in that flea rinse? Blokes don't read *books*.

SANDY
I just mean this could be a positive thing for you. A change. A new beginning. Our life was getting stale, anyway.

LORRY
Stale? I know you're trying to put a positive spin on this luv but-

SANDY
I'm not. I just think it could be time to find the rest of yer life, Lorry.

LORRY
Whaddya mean?

SANDY
(sings)

"COME FIND THE REST OF YOUR LIFE LORRY
HARRIGAN"

EAT THAT BREAKFAST PIE
YOU'LL BE LATE FOR WORK
CHECK THE TRUCK AND SIGH
THE BOSS IS SUCH A JERK
THAT'S BIZ, LORRY
BUT IS THIS ALL THERE IS, LORRY?
COME FIND THE REST OF YOUR LIFE

DRIVERS IN YOUR LANE
PAPER BY YOUR SIDE
CURSING AT THE RAIN
ANOTHER SOGGY RIDE
BACK HOME
BOSS IS ON THE PHONE, LORRY
COME FIND THE REST OF YOUR LIFE

COME
COME TASTE THE MUSIC OF LIFE, LORRY
TO YOURSELF YOU HUM
A SWEET MELODY ALL YOUR LIFE
LISTEN TO YOUR BLOODY WIFE, LORRY

TUESDAY COMES ALONG
GATHER ROUND THE BAR
SAME OLD JOKES AND SONGS
MONDAY SEEMS SO FAR
AWAY
CHANGE YOUR LIFE TODAY, LORRY
COME FIND THE REST OF YOUR LIFE

(INSTRUMENTAL BREAK)

LIVE
LIVE EVERY DAY AS YOUR LAST, LORRY
TO YOURSELF YOU GIVE
CAUSE LIFE IS A PLAY WHICH YOU CAST,
LORRY
STOP IT RUNNING PAST, LORRY

SATURDAY IS PAIN
HOLD YOUR ACHING HEAD
PILLS TO NUMB YOUR BRAIN
WHY GET OUT OF BED
NO NEED, LORRY
BUT A SOUL'S A THING TO FEED, LORRY
COME FIND THE REST OF
THE NORTH, EAST AND WEST OF
COME FIND THE REST OF YOUR LIFE
LORRY.

Graham enters the stage, smoking a cigarette and drinking a glass of whiskey.

LORRY
(to Graham)
Since when did you take up smoking?

GRAHAM
(flatly)
About five minutes ago.

SANDY
Why?

GRAHAM

Well, I'm not in training anymore. Thought I'd push the boat out.

Lorry paces.

LORRY
Well, I'm not taking all this lying down. Sandy, Graham, watch this space.

TRANSITION TO:

INT. RADIO STUDIO - DAY

The stage is dark. We see a giant slide of Jesus wearing a set of recording headphones.

In the darkness we hear conversation.

HALLSY (V.O.)
On the line we have Lorry from Gosford. Let's hear how King Baird is driving people to suicide with the imminent shut-down of the dog racing industry. Let's examine how Baird's, order, his decree, his autocratic declaration, (poco crescendo) his Stalinist, Chairman Mao Tse-tung edict, effects the Little Battler. So let's hear from the Voice of the Voiceless. The man in Struggle Street.
Good morning, Lorry.

LORRY (V.O.)
Um...hello? Is that you, Hallsy?

HALLSY (V.O.)
Yes. You're on air, Lorry.

LORRY (V.O.)
I'm actually live on air? On the wireless?

HALLSY (V.O.)
Yes, go ahead caller. You're obliviously a man from Struggle Street.

LORRY (V.O.)
No.

HALLSY (V.O.)
Really? My producer said-

LORRY (V.O.)
I live on Mullet Drive, West Gosford.

HALLSY (V.O.)
(sighs)
No, I meant... never mind. Tell the listeners how this dog racing ban affects you, Lorry. I bet you feel like topping yourself, right?

LORRY (V.O.)
Not really. Nothing's worth that, Hallsy.

HALLSY (V.O.)
But my producer said dog racing is your entire life.

LORRY (V.O.)
Oh sure. But killing yerself over a sport is a bit over the top, Hallsy. For instance, when North Sydney got dropped from the league, me mate Showbags-

HALLSY (V.O.)
Showbags?

LORRY (V.O.)
Yeah, we call him that cause he's fuller nuthun but shit.

We hear dialtone.

LORRY (V.O.) (cont'd)
Hello...? Hallsy...? *Hellooo*...?

TRANSITION TO:

INT. FELICITY BLISS'S FLAT GOSFORD - LATER

Felicity is chatting with her mother, TABATHA (50s, funky clothes, middle-class accent).

Felicity makes a pot of tea.

FELICITY
You don't understand, mother. The tabloid media is putting tremendous pressure on Baird to reverse the ban. PeTa thinks he'll buckle.

TABATHA
Darling, don't be ridiculous. Soon you'll be saying Trump will be the next American President.

FELICITY
Now, who's being ridiculous?

They both laugh.

TABATHA
Reversing Baird's decision would be political suicide.

FELICITY

Problem is, it might just be if he doesn't. That's what worries us at peTA.

TABATHA
(drinking)
Nobody takes the tabloids seriously, Darling. Anyone with half a brain reads the Herald or the Guardian on-line. What *is* this appalling drink?

FELICITY
Herbal tea.

TABATHA
Horrible tea?

Felicity pins her with a look.

FELICITY
How many people outside the inner-city read the Herald or watch the ABC, Mum? I'm telling you, this tabloid hysteria is building like a tidal wave. It's a worry.

TABATHA
You're over-thinking it as usual, Darling.

FELICITY
I wish it were true, Mother. It's what the tabloids and the shock-jocks *aren't* saying that's the problem. To bolster ratings, they conveniently neglect to mention that the industry is fraught with corruption, over-breeding, and the use of illegal drugs.

TABATHA
Sounds like a family from Paddington I know.

FELICITY

Mum, this is *serious*!

TABATHA
Sorry darling. (pulling a face at the tea) Why can't we have Twinings?

FELICITY
Because - as I've told you countless times Mother - the commercial tea trade is all about exploiting people from the Third World. In some cases children as young as five-years-old are picking the tea you drink at home.

TABATHA
But they have such tiny fingers, Darling. What else would they do? There's no Nintendo, bless.

FELICITY
Now *you're* being flippant. I know you don't mean that.

TABATHA
(sipping tea, puling face)
Of course not. Might I just have some hot water, Darling.

FELICITY
Again?? You always ask for hot water when you visit. Are you detoxing?

Felicity exits the stage with Tabatha's cup.

TABATHA
Not quite. So tell me about this new boy you're seeing.

FELICITY (O.S.)
Well, we met at the beach. He loves greyhounds. I love greyhounds. You know...

TABATHA
What does he do?

Felicity enters the stage with a cup of hot water.

FELICITY
I think he said he's a "hip-rocker".

TABATHA
A musician? He doesn't have tattoos, does he Darling?
I'm so *ooover* tattoos.

FELICITY
What does it matter?

TABATHA
Or those horrible piercings, Darling? You know, where
they stretch their earlobes like a whore's tuppence?

FELICITY
Mum! Anyway, who cares if he has tattoos or piercings?

TABATHA
I do, Darling! What is it with all these first-world kids
trying to look tribal? Believe me, people in the Amazon
are buying plasma TVs and iPhones. They should send
these tribal hipsters to live in a rainforest for a year -
without their lattes and quinoa.

FELICITY
I've seen old photos of you with a nose ring.

TABATHA
That was the 80s, Darling. And it was tiny.

FELICITY

Anyway, we have our first official date on Friday night. Not sure what to wear. It might be a fancy restaurant. It might be a music venue. God! Then I'll be overdressed.

TABATHA
I'll come to his gig. I *live* to dance and embarrass you. You know that, Darling. Do you have a biscuit for Mummy's hot water?

They both laugh. Felicity exits.

We see Tabatha remove a tea bag from her handbag and dunk it in the cup before hiding the evidence.

FELICITY (O.S.)
How was the Fellini Film Festival, last week?

TABATHA
Wonderful, Darling. Wonderful! Bruno was there. He sends his love. Rather think he fancies you. He's always asking after you.

Felicity returns.

FELICITY
Yes me and 1500 other women. That's the problem.

TABATHA
Once you've tasted Italian, Darling...

FELICITY
I've decided to try some local produce for a change.

TABATHA
Your Gosford hip-rocker.

FELICITY
Perhaps.

TABATHA
Well, I'll have to pounce on him myself. I'll sprinkle
downstairs with a little Parmesan.

FELICITY
(open-mouthed)
Mum! You're such a wicked cougar!

TABATHA
You bet I am! Oh, I'm seeing the new Ben Quilty
exhibition next week. I've commissioned a work from
him, you know. Mates rates, of course.

FELICITY
Commissioned a painting? Mum, you're such a culture
vulture.

TABATHA
Culture is my middle name, Darling. (Tabatha sings)

"CULTURE VULTURE"

I'M A CULTURE VULTURE LADY
I DRIVE A PINK MERCEDES
ABREAST OF EVERY FASHION
HAD AN NOSE-RING IN THE EIGHTIES
I'M AT EVERY ARTY FESTIVAL
I'LL CONTEMPLATE A TESTICLE
CULTURE IS MY MIDDLE NAME

I'M A CULTURE VULTURE FELLOW
ONCE I OWNED A CELLO

ANY FOOD I'LL TRY IT
IF YOU'RE QUICK I'LL BUY IT
FOREIGN FLICKS
AND POLITICS
I BUY MY ART WITH ENORMOUS DICKS
CULTURE IS MY MIDDLE NAME

I'M TALKING ABOUT STYLE
PADDED SHOULDERS WERE IN FOR A WHILE
NOW THEY'RE OUT AND FLARES ARE IN
AND A PAIR OF FLARES WITH TEARS IS NOW
THE THING

I'M A CULTURE VULTURE BABY
THE QUEEN OF THE LADIES
AN ULTRA CULTURED FELLOW
OH JAZZ JUST MAKES ME MELLOW
SAMBUCCA IS MY TIPPLE
I'VE EVEN PIERCED MY NIPPLE
CULTURE IS MY MIDDLE NAME

I'M TALKIN BOUT COOL
I'M TALKIN PADDINGTON PARTAYS
I'M NOBODY'S FOOL
SO I DRAW THE LINE AT CHAI LATTES

I'M A CULTURE VULTURE LASSIE
MARTINIS MAKE ME SASSY
AN ULTRA CULTURED SISTER
A V.I.P. A-LISTER
MY CAVIAR'S BELUGA
I'M AN CULTURED SULTRY COUGAR
CULTURE IS MY MIDDLE NAME
(FELICITY) DON'T BE LAME

CULTURE IS MY MIDDLE NAME
(FELICITY) YOU'RE INSANE
CULTURE IS MY MIDDLE NAME
FAME!

TRANSITION TO:

INT. RADIO STUDIO - DAY

The stage is dark. We again see a giant slide of Jesus in headphones.

In the darkness we hear conversation.

HALLSY (V.O.)
On the line we have Felicity. Felicity's one of these people who actually *supports* the greyhound racing ban. Can you believe it, listeners? Felicity's one of those people who are happy to see good folk thrown out of work. Happy to see families torn apart. Happy to see people moving interstate. Delighted to see people committing suicide. Let's hear what Felicity has to say. Good morning, Felicity.

FELICITY (V.O.)
Nice to hear a balanced view, Hallsy.

HALLSY (V.O.)
I'm entitled to an opinion, Sweetheart.

FELICITY (V.O.)
Don't call me Sweetheart. It's patronising.

HALLSY (V.O.)
Oh I'm sorry, Darling.

FELICITY (V.O.)
Don't call me, Darling. Only my mother calls me, Darling.

HALLSY (V.O.)
Okay sorry sweetheart. What have you got to say about the ban?

FELICITY (V.O.)
Don't call me sweetheart. Don't call me darling. As your producer told you, my name is Felicity.

HALLSY (V.O.)
You're calling my program. I'll call you what I want, Sweetheart.

FELICITY (V.O.)
Why do you only call women "sweetheart" or "darling", Hallsy? Why not men?

HALLSY (V.O.)
Okay, I won't call you sweetheart or darling. Happy?

FELICITY (V.O.)
Thank you.

HALLSY (V.O.)
Now, what's you're point, lovely.

FELICITY (V.O.)
Arghhh!

We hear dial tone.

TRANSITION TO:

INT. HARRIGAN FAMILY HOME GOSFORD - DAY

Sandy is ironing a series of blue singlets, blue shorts,
blues socks.

SANDY
(aside)
Some days ironing really gives me the blues.

Lorry enters the stage full of excitement.

LORRY
Sandy, I've been thinking.

SANDY
(aside)
Sounds dangerous.

LORRY
How long have we lived in Gosford?

SANDY
(ironing)
Ever since I moved down from Dunedoo. Twenny years
or so. Why?

LORRY
I reckon we need a change!

SANDY
(ironing)
Why?

LORRY

Start anew. Refresh our love for each other. Just the two of us. The boys are old enough to look after themselves, now. Let's *downsize*.

Sandy plonks down the iron.

SANDY
(excited)
That's what I was trying to tell you! A new life.

LORRY
Well, you're absolutely right!

SANDY
(suspicious)
Haaang on...where is our romantic new life gunner be situated exactly?

Lorry unfolds a series of brochures.

LORRY
The Gold Coast!

SANDY
Bloody Queensland??

LORRY
I've been talkin' with Charlie about it.

SANDY
Charlie?? Yer brother, Charlie?? That shonky bastard. I'm not gettin' mixed up in *anything* he's involved in.

LORRY
Steady on, Luv. He's changed. He's very well respected these days. Last year he got an AO.

SANDY
(cynically)
Yeah, Order of Arseholes.

LORRY
That's a bit harsh, Luv. He got the AO for his charity
work.

SANDY
Yeah, because it's a tax dodge.

LORRY
You've never got over him dumping you, did ya?

SANDY
Dumping me?? I dumped him for you, fool.

LORRY
So you say.

SANDY
Don't you get it?? He think's he's so much better than us.
He's nothing but a cashed-up bogan. And I told him so
at Chook's wedding.

LORRY
Anyway, we're getting off track. What does Charlie do
for a living?

SANDY
Professional swindler.

LORRY
Sandy, be serious. He's a property developer.

SANDY

Is that what they call it these days.

LORRY
Will you be *serious*? He can get a us a deal on a
Southport apartment on the Gold Coast.

SANDY
On a disused swamp?

LORRY
That's just mean. Look, Sandy. Let's blow this popsicle
stand. Let's find romance again. Love. Let's fly away!

SANDY
Fly away?

LORRY
(sings)
  "LET'S FLY AWAY"

(VERSE) GOSFORD'S RATHER DULL
IN WINTER TIME
AND OUR LOVE HAS BEGUN TO FEEL LIKE
SPRING
AND I HAVE JUST BEGUN TO SING

LET'S FLY AWAY
AND FIND A DAY
THAT'S OURS ALONE
JUST LIKE TODAY
LET'S PULL THE PIN
I'LL GIVE A SHOVE
LET'S FALL IN LOVE!

LET'S FLY AWAY

LET'S START ANEW
A BRAND NEW LIFE
JUST ME AND YOU
LET'S FLY AWAY
IN SKIES ABOVE
LET'S FALL IN LOVE!

ROME IS HIP
PARIS IS PRETTY
BUT I'VE GOT MY HEART SET ON GOLD COAST
CITY
THEY'LL THINK US RASH
AND RATHER RUDE
TO LEAVE OUR LIVES
FOR AN INTERLUDE
WE'LL JUST START OUR LIVES ANEW
IN A SOUTHPORT APARTMENT
BUILT FOR TWO
AND WE'LL FORGET
THE LIVES WE LEFT BEHIND

LET'S FLY AWAY
AND KISS GOODBYE
A CRAZY WORLD
FROM HIGH IN THE SKY
I'LL PAWN MY WATCH
YOU HOCK SOME STUFF
LET'S FALL IN LOVE!

(INSTRUMENTAL BREAK - LORRY AND SANDY
DANCE)

ROME IS HIP
PARIS IS PRETTY
BUT I'VE GOT MY HEART SET ON GOLD COAST

CITY
THEY'LL THINK US RASH
AND RATHER RUDE
TO LEAVE OUR LIVES
FOR A ROMANTIC INTERLUDE
WE'LL JUST START OUR LIVES ANEW
IN A SOUTHPORT APARTMENT
BUILT FOR TWO
AND WE'LL FORGET
THE LIVES WE LEFT BEHIND

LET'S FLY AWAY
AND KISS GOODBYE
THIS P.C. WORLD
FROM HIGH IN THE SKY
I'LL PAWN MY WATCH
YOU FLOG SOME STUFF
CAUSE QUEENSLAND'S THE PLACE WHERE
DREAMS ARE MADE OF
LET'S FLY AWAY
IN SKIES ABOVE
LET'S FALL IN LOVE!

SANDY
(suspiciously)
Haang on...this romantic Gold Coast Apartment for
two... It wouldn't be anywhere near the Parklands
Greyhound Racing track, would it?

LORRY
(nervously)
By coincidence, the apartment overlooks the track!

Sandy folds her arms and pins Lorry with a look.

EXT. GOSFORD SHOWGROUND RACE TRACK - NIGHT

Lorry, Showbags and Beer Bottle are picking dogs and sucking on beers at the track.

SHOWBAGS
Any more news about moving to the Gold Coast, Loz?

LORRY
(excitedly)
No.

SHOWBAGS
Changed yer mind?

LORRY
Nah, Sandy wouldn't go for it. Her mum is here and she's frail. And she has her business. But mate, did you read the Tele this morning?

BEER BOTTLE
Loz, you know Showbags can't read.

LORRY
Can't you read, Bags?

SHOWBAGS
Nup. I'm belligerent.

A beat. Beer Bottle and Lorry exchange glances.

LORRY

Well, Sandy thinks there's a real groundswell building against the ban. Everyday there's something in the Tele about the injustice of the ban. Baird must be feeling the pressure. Sandy sees a glimmer of light at the end of the rainbow. We gotta stay and fight it out! Write to the papers an that. Write to our local MP. I've been calling up the radio.

BEER BOTTLE
Mate, I know dogs are yer life and I hate to be a Negative Nancy but the Premier's never gunna reverse his decision in a million years, Lorry. It doesn't work like that, Champion.

SHOWBAGS
(nodding)
Beer Bottle's, right. It'd be political suicide, mate.

LORRY
Sandy reckons it might be if he doesn't but.

SHOWBAGS
Hey, changing the subject, how's the young bloke goin with his new bird?

LORRY
Getting quite serious. She coming to dinner next week. He's quite nervous about it.

BEER BOTTLE
She'll only break his heart. First love always does. Laws of nature.

LORRY
Now, who's being a Negative Nancy?

SHOWBAGS
Bottle never got over this first great love.

LORRY
That's right she was a real beauty in her day, wasn't she,
mate? Remember that old photo of her at the Entrance
Mardigras?

BEER BOTTLE
Yeah, wore a beautiful purple sash that read: *Miss
Entrance 1975.*

A beat. Lorry and Bags on cue look aside to the
audience.

LORRY
She was a bit older than you, if I recall.

BEER BOTTLE
Yeah, these days you'd call her a "cougar". But that was
before Courtney Cox had the TV show. We didn't have
that word back then.

LORRY
(looking askance at Showbags)
I mean...there was quite an age difference...

Lorry and Showbags exchange clandestine looks.

BEER BOTTLE
Sure. Sure. But you don't see age when you're in love.
But it turned out I was just a passing fling to her,
anyway. She was always outta my league.

SHOWBAGS

Ewes lived together in a caravan park in Budgewoi, if I recall.

BEER BOTTLE
Yeah. Still get a pang when I drive past the old caravan park. We had our last kiss in that caravan.

LORRY
How did you meet this beautful cougar, exactly?

BEER BOTTLE
(sings)

"SHE SAID GOODBYE IN BUDGEWOI"

WHEN I WAS A YOUNG MAN
ONLY JUST EIGHTEEN
I MET A PRETTY LADY
A FORMER BEAUTY QUEEN
SHE LED ME TO HER CARAVAN
WHERE SHE STOLE AWAY MY YOUTH
OUR ROMANCE LASTED EIGHTEEN MONTHS
UNTIL SHE SPILLED THE TRUTH
I WAS JUST A FLING SHE SAID
A THING NOT MEANT TO LAST
BUT WAS I JUST *THE GRADUATE*?
A FAD YOU HATE SO FAST?

OH SHE SAID GOODBYE IN BUDGEWOI
THAT'S WHERE SHE BROKE THE NEWS
IN HER LAWNBOWL WHITES
AND SURGICAL TIGHTS
AND SILENT SHOES

OH SHE SAID GOODBYE IN BUDGEWOI

AFTER STOPPING CALLS
SO NO MORE ADVENTURES
WITH MY TONGUE IN HER DENTURES
IN SHOPPING MALLS

OH YES I WAS BEDAZZLED
BY HER VAGAZZLED UNDERCROFT
BUT WHILE HER
MINGE WAS SHORN
WELL BEFORE I WAS BORN
IT WAS DOILY SOFT

OH SHE SAID GOODBYE IN BUDGEWOI
I'LL MISS HER FUNNY WAYS
I'LL MISS HER GLARES AT THE LOCALS
THROUGH PAIRS OF BI-FOCALS
HER ROMANTIC LINGO
WHISPERED THROUGH BINGO
(ALL) OH WHY, OH WHY,
DID SHE SAY GOODBYE
IN BUDGEWOI?

OH SHE SAID GOODBYE IN BUDGEWOI
I'LL MISS HER MOTHBALL SCENT
BENEATH HER SEXUAL ARSENAL
WITH HER TEETH IN A GLASS-FULL
OF POLIDENT

OH SHE SAID GOODBYE IN BUDGEWOI
I'LL MISS HER HOME-COOKED FOOD
I'LL MISS HER KNITTING ME CARDIS
WHILE SCULLING BACARDIS
AND BAKING NUDE

OH YES I WAS ENAMOURED

OF GETTING QUITE HAMMERED
ON JACOB'S CREEK
AND FRISKY WITH YOUR LICKS
ON WHISKEY AND HORLICKS
AT SENIOR'S WEEK.

OH SHE SAID GOODBYE IN BUDGEWOI
I'LL MISS HER CROOKED SMILE
I'LL MISS HER LOW SWINGING HOOTERS
ON MOBILITY SCOOTERS
HER SIX-O'CLOCK TIPPLE
HER LONG SAGGING NIPPLE
OH WOI OH WOI
DID SHE SAY GOODBYE
IN BUDGEWOI?
OH WOI OH WOI
DID SHE SAY GOODBYE
IN BUDGEWOI?

TRANSITION TO:

EXT. GOSFORD SHOWGROUND - NIGHT

We see Lorry, Showbags and Bottle studying the form-guide at the track, whilst sucking on beers.

BEER BOTTLE
Nice night. No rain.

LORRY
You know what that means tomorrow?

THE BOYS
Slugs.

LORRY
(looking up at night sky)
  Yep. Garden'll be full of slugs.

BEER BOTTLE
What is a slug but a snail living on the street?

SHOWBAGS
I know the feeling.

BEER BOTTLE
Me too. Been losing me shirt on Graham every week.
What's going *on*?

LORRY
What can I tell ya? He's lost his mojo, boys.

SHOWBAGS
Mate, last time we spoke you were going to race
Graham in the big one at Sandown.

LORRY
Yeah but Graham's taken the news about the racing ban
very badly. He's on the lung-busters, he's eating donuts,
not exercising. Just given up. Lost his drive.

BEER BOTTLE
Do you think he might need to visit he-who-shall-not-
be-named?

LORRY
Live-baiting Lionel? Mate, you're not serious?

SHOWBAGS
Mate, we're deadly serious. Bags and I think he needs an
edge. I mean, if you're gunner front the coin and

everything for Sandown. You can't compete if the other dogs have all been blooded. It's not a level playing field. What would Sandy say if yer blew it all on a dud dog?

LORRY
(apoplectic)
But don't you *see*?? It's blokes like Lionel that have knifed our sport!?? It's not the Greenies. It's not the ABC. It's not even, Baird. It's low pricks like Lionel.

CHARLIE (60's, smart suit jacket, white thongs, gold chains) enters and loiters side-stage, in deep (mimed) conversation on his mobile.

Showbags nudges Lorry.

SHOWBAGS
Mate, isn't that your brother, Charlie, over there.

LORRY
(reading form guide, not looking up)
My brother? Yeah, right. Race horses, sure. Dogs? Never. He wouldn't be seen dead-

Lorry looks up. Charlie waves from the corner of the stage.

SHOWBAGS
Just gunner put a trifecta on.

BEER BOTTLE
Yeah, we'll see you after Graham runs, Loz. Hope he goes okay. Bags and me have each got an avocado on the snout on him tonight.

LORRY

Fifty bucks?!

Showbags and Beer Bottle exit, leaving the brothers to chat.

CHARLIE
(to phone)
Mate, I'll call you back. (to Lorry - shaking hands). Hello little brother!

LORRY
When did you get here, Charlie?

CHARLIE
Flew in last night.

LORRY
(stunned)
What a *wonderful* surprise! Great to see you. Did you get my message? Sandy's not keen on moving to the Gold Coast, I'm afraid. We'll have to give that apartment a miss. Is that why you're here?

CHARLIE
No, I thought I'd get involved in the dog racing before it all ends. For the Old Man, you know..didn't the Old Man love the dishlickers? Bless him.

LORRY
Dogs were his life. That, and fishing.

CHARLIE
Yeah, we spent so much time at this dog track as kids I grew to hate the joint. Embarrassed. But I've had a change of heart. (looking around) How many acres is this site, you reckon?

LORRY
Dunno. Never thought about it, really. Quite a lot I'd
say. Why?

CHARLIE
Ahh nothing. Hey, how are my fabulous nephews?

LORRY
Mate, fantastic. They're here tonight. They'd love to see
you. Gary finished uni. He's a vet now. And Warwick's
in love. Long story. And how's Kylie, yer new wife?
She was your Au Pair, wasn't she?

CHARLIE
Yeah, you should see her now. Bought her a new set of
tits for her birthday. Tell a lie, (nudges Lorry) for "my
birthday", ha ha.

LORRY
(pointing to his teeth)
Does she still have braces?

CHARLIE
Had em off last year. Beautiful teeth now. Speaking of
crooked teeth, how's Sandy?

LORRY
(awkardly)
Good. Good mate. Look Charlie, I'm sorry about last
time - the blue ewes had at Chook's wedding. Bloody
terrible.

CHARLIE
Forget it. We were all pissed. I don't even know what
that was about, to be honest.

LORRY
Well, you did call her a feral pig-shooting bush mole.
Bit harsh, mate. She *is* me wife.

CHARLIE
Did I? That's the piss talking. Sorry about that, little
brother. Remember what she called *me*?

LORRY
Can't remember. I was pissed, too. We all were. Bundy
shots. Never again. What did she call you?

CHARLIE
A "boganaire".

LORRY
(flatly)
Did she? Shit. Sorry about that.

CHARLIE
No no its fine! Fine! In fact, I've embraced the moniker.
Hey, I'm in pretty good company: Clive Palmer, Nathan
Tinkler, James Packer. I even now have personalised
number plates that read *Boganaire.*

LORRY
Really? What does it even *mean*?

CHARLIE
Well, it's an amalgam-

LORRY
What's amalgam mean?

CHARLIE

Combination. Mixture. It's a combination of the word "Bogan" and "Millionaire". Or in Packer's case "Billionaire". "Boganaire". Get it?

LORRY
Now, I remember! The *Daily Telegraph* called him that when he punched on in Bondi, that time.

CHARLIE
That's right! They even had a fashion page on what a Boganaire wears.

LORRY
(pointing, noticing)
That's the watch!

CHARLIE
Exactly. (Charlie sings)

"BOGANAIRE"

WEAR ME THONGS OUT
WHILE I DRINK THE BEST OF VINO
PULL ME SHLONG OUT
AT ANY RESTAURANT OR CASINO
DON'T CARE
I'M A BOGANAIRE

IN ME LEAR JET
WHILE I'M MOSTLY PISSED AND FUNNY
IT'S A CLEAR BET
I'LL SHAG A HOSTY IN THE DUNNY
(LORRY) AND THE AU PAIR
(CHARLIE) AND THE AU PAIR

I'M A BOGANAIRE

CATCH YOU DOWN AT BONDI
WHERE IT MIGHT BE NICE TO MEET
I'LL TAKE YOU FOR A SCHOONER
THEN I'LL FIGHT YOU IN THE STREET
DON'T CARE
WHO STARES
I SWEAR
I'M A BOGANAIRE

IN ME LABELS
I'M THE FACE AT ALL THE COURSES
AT ME STABLES
YOU CAN TAKE YER PICK OF HORSES
(LORRY) AND SHAG THE MARE
(CHARLIE) AND SHAG THE MARE
I'M A BOGANAIRE

CATCH YOU DOWN AT BONDI
WHERE IT MIGHT BE NICE TO MEET
I'LL TAKE YOU FOR A SCHOONER
THEN I'LL FIGHT YOU IN THE STREET
DON'T CARE
WHO STARES
I SWEAR
I'M A BOGANAIRE

I'M A BOOZER
I'M A SORTA BACCHANALIAN
I'M A SCHMOOZER
(LORRY) WON THE ORDER OF AUSTRALIA
(CHARLIE) OH YEAH!
I'M A BOGANAIRE

(INSTRUMENTAL BREAK - CAST DANCE)

CATCH ME ON THE GOLF COURSE
WHERE I MOSTLY SWING AND MISS
MEET YA AT THE CLUB HOUSE
FIRST I NEED TO TAKE A PISS
(LORRY) RIGHT THERE?
DON'T CARE
WHO STARES
I'M A FREAKIN' BOGANAIRE

We hear Charlie's ring-tone which is ABBA's *Money Money Money*.

CHARLIE (cont'd)
Loz, I'll need to take this call.

LORRY
Right you are, Charlie. I'll go find the boys. Wait till I tell them you're here. They'll love to see you.

Lorry exits the stage.

CHARLIE
(conspiratorially into phone)
Mate, this shit heap is a bloody gold mine. You could build a thousand townhouses on this site. After the "home for abused greyhounds", of course, ha ha.

TRANSITION TO:

INT. HARRIGAN FAMILY HOME GOSFORD - NIGHT

The Harrigans (sans Lorry and Sandy at BBQ off-stage) wait anxiously at the dinner table for their special guest.

Graham is reading Solzhenitsyn on the floor.

GARY
She works for Peter, you say? Peter Thompson? Thomo? At the dog track?

WARWICK
Yeah. Well...at least I think so.

GARY
You worked for Peter, right?

WARWICK
Yeah. Top bloke, Pete. Always believed in me. Said I could be anything. Once told me I could be Obama.

SANDY (O.S.)
He said you could be a *barman*. You know...pouring drinks at the track.

Warwick is defeated.

Lorry enters stage-right - wearing a chef's hat and a BBQ apron with kitsch bikini-clad motif. He clutches long tongs like an Olympic Torch.

Sandy follows with a tiny salad.

We hear a DOORBELL RING.

WARWICK
She's here! She's here!!

Warwick runs off stage-left.

LORRY
Now, don't seem too eager mate! Treat em mean, keep em keen, I always say.

SANDY
Excuse me?

LORRY
(anxiously)
Sorry, luv. Not you, of course. I've seen you drop a bloke in a bar with a left-hook.

SANDY
(remembering)
He went down like a sack of doorknobs. I kept drinking schooners with me right-hand, but.

Felicity enters stage-left, cradling a bottle of wine.

There is a horrified moment of recognition between Sandy and Felicity.

WARWICK
Dad, Gary, this is Felicity.

LORRY
Nice to meet yer, luvvy.

WARWICK
Mum, this is-

SANDY
(dryly)
We've met.

WARWICK
Really??

FELICITY
(dryly)
I'm one of your Mum's clients.

SANDY
(soto voce)
Was. (To Felicity) Your greyhound is Lolita, right?

FELICITY
Yes.

GRAHAM
(in ecstasy)
Lolita, light of my life, fire of my loins. My sin, my
soul. Lo-lee-ta: the tip of the tongue taking a trip of
three steps down the palate to tap, at three, on the teeth.

WARWICK
Of course you know Graham from the beach.

GRAHAM
(to Felicity)
How's my special girl? Tell her I adored the Tolstoy she
sent me. Couldn't put it down. I'm reading so much I'm
getting a Kindle.

Felicity looks around and notices all the dog racing
paraphernalia with impending horror. It's all making
sense to her now. She looks at Warwick. She looks at
Sandy.

LORRY

How do yer like your steaks, luv? Got half a cow on the hot plate with *your* name on it.

SANDY
(flatly)
She's a vegetarian.

FELICITY
(nodding, stunned)
I'm a vegetarian.

WARWICK
How'd you know that, Mum?

SANDY
(dryly)
Lucky guess.

LORRY
Well, that'll have to change, young lady. Can't have any future daughter-in-law-

WARWICK
Daaad!

LORRY
Okay okay...girlfriend of me son's lacking iron, now can we? How will yer squirt out me grand-kids with no iron in yer? We need to introduce you to the wonderful world of *meat*!

GRAHAM
(aside)
I'm with him. Have you ever met a dog who says, "sorry I'm a vegetarian"?

LORRY
We didn't fight our way up the food chain to eat bean
sprouts. Right boys?

GARY
(chuckling)
We eat a lot of meat in this house, Felicity. It'd make a
Buddhist blush.

LORRY
Ever tired meat? Why not have a go tonight! We've got
all types of meat in the freezer. It's a bloody zoo in
there. It's just about finding the right kind of meat for
you, I reckon!

Lorry, Warwick, Gary and Graham sing at Felicity -
with Graham's asides to the audience.

Sandy remains silent and frosty.

"MEAT SONG"

(LORRY) TRY YOUR LUCK,
(WARWICK) WITH SOME DUCK,
(ALL) STICK YOUR FORK INTO SOME PORK
UNTIL YOU CHUCK,
(WARWICK) TRY SOME HAM,
(LORRY) I'VE A LITTLE LEG OF LAMB INSIDE,
(ALL) CAUSE NOTHING TASTES AS SWEET,
AS EATING GREAT BIG SLABS OF MEAT.

(WARWICK) SECOND COURSE,
(LORRY) TRY SOME HORSE,

(ALL) TRY A CHUNKY LITTLE MONKEY AS A
SAUCE,
(GARY) NO REMORSE!
(LORRY) CAUSE YOU'D BE MENTAL EATING
LENTILS,
(ALL) AFTER TENDER TREATS
AS SWEET AS MEAT.

(LORRY) YOU'LL FEEL STRONGER
(WARWICK) YOU'LL FEEL GREAT,
(GARY) YOU'LL FEEL PURE ELATION,
(WARWICK) YOU'LL LIVE LONGER,
(LORRY) YOU'LL GAIN WEIGHT,
(GRAHAM - ASIDE) AND MINOR CONSTIPATION.

(LORRY) TRY SOME VEAL,
(WARWICK) WITH YOUR MEAL,
(GARY) OR LIKE THE ESKIMOS A NOSE OF
SEAL,
(LORRY) TRY SOME EEL,
(WARWICK) LIKE IT RARE? KOALA BEAR?
(ALL) CAUSE NOTHING TASTES AS SWEET AS
EATING MEAT.

(KEY CHANGE)

(LORRY) TRY SOME ROO,
(WARWICK) TRY IT BLEUE,
(GARY) OR TRY ALBINO RHINO (LORRY) TRY
THE ZOO!
(WARWICK) EMU STEW?
(LORRY) THERE'S NO SENTIMENTAL
ORIENTALS,
(ALL) NOTHING TASTES AS SWEET
AS EATING FOOD THAT WALKED THE STREET.

(LORRY) FOR A LAUGH,
(WARWICK) TRY GIRAFFE,
(GARY) OR LIKE THE ARGENTINES OF MEANS
THE CALF,
(WARWICK) TRY JUST HALF,
(GRAHAM) ONLY SLIGHTLY HUNG QUEENS
LIVE ON MUNG BEANS,
(ALL) NOTHING'S IS AS SWEET AS EATING
MEAT.

(LORRY) MEAT'S IS GOOD,
(WARWICK) MEAT'S IS FINE,
(GARY) MEAT IS JUST THE ANSWER,
(WARWICK) MEAT IS TOPS,
(LORRY) GREAT WITH WINE,
(GRAHAM - ASIDE) BUT WATCH FOR COLON
CANCER,

(LORRY) TRY SOME QUAIL,
(WARWICK) TRY SOME SNAIL,
(GARY) IN CINCINNATI THEY LIKE FATTY
WHALE,
(WARWICK) LOBSTER TAIL?
(LORRY) OR TRY SOME POODLE WITH YOUR
NOODLE?
(GRAHAM) HEY!!!
(ALL) NOTHING TASTES AS SWEET AS EATING
MEAT.

(KEY CHANGE)

(LORRY) TRY SOME HOG,
(WARWICK) TRY A FROG,

(GARY) OR LIKE THE PEKINESE SOME CHEESE AND DOG,
(WARWICK) I'M AGOG,
(LORRY) THAT YOU'D CHOOSE BIRD SEED OVER HERD STEED,
(ALL) YOU NEVER FEEL REPLETE,
UNTIL YOU EAT GREAT CHUNKS OF MEAT

(LORRY) NOW FOR FAT,
(WARWICK) TRY SOME BAT,
(GARY) OR LIKE THE DUTCH A CLUTCH OF MALTESE CAT,
(WARWICK) OR WOMBAT,
(LORRY) WILL MAKE YOUR HAIR SHINE LIKE A BOVINE,
(ALL) CAUSE NOTHING TASTES AS SWEET AS EATING MEAT.

(LORRY) MEAT IS COOL,
(WARWICK) MEAT IS NOW,
(GARY) BEANS ARE FOR THE FOOLS,
(WARWICK) MEAT IS SMART,
(LORRY) ASK A COW,
(GRAHAM - ASIDE) ENJOY THOSE ROCK-HARD STOOLS.

(LORRY) TRY SOME OWL,
(WARWICK) TRY SOME FOWL,
(GARY) AND LIKE THE FILIPINOS WE KNOWS HOW,
(WARWICK) DON'T YOU SCOWL,
(LORRY) SWEDES LIKE FEEDS OF CENTIPEDES CAUSE,
(ALL) THERE'S NO FOOD THAT'S FINER,
YOU'RE THE CONSUMMATE FINE DINER

YOU'RE THE APEX OF THE FOOD CHAIN,
(LORRY) YOU'RE THE KING,
(WARWICK) YOU'RE THE BOSS,
(GARY) YOU'LL FEEL PROUD,
(GRAHAM) YOU'LL FEEL FRESH,
(ALL) OH, WELCOME TO OUR HUMBLE WORLD
OF...
(ALL - INCLUDING ORCHESTRA) FLESH!

FELICITY
(stunned, upset)
I've left my phone in the car.

Felicity dashes from the stage.

WARWICK
(calling after her)
What about fish? Do you like mullet?

LORRY
How about a sausage? There's hardly any meat in em.
Mostly lips and arseholes.

SANDY
She won't be eating a mullet. Or sausages. Idiots! In
fact, she's not coming back.

LORRY
Whaddya mean?

WARWICK
How do you know so much about her, anyway?

SANDY

(furious)
  Don't you get it?

WARWICK
Get what?

SANDY
She's one of *them*!

LORRY
A lesbo?

GARY
(winking)
  That's why she's a vegetarian.

WARWICK
Mum, I don't want to go into details but I assure you
she's not. We've been pretty intimate...

LORRY
(winking to Gary)
  Hey, that's my boy! In like Flynn!

SANDY
No. Not a lesbian. She works for peTA!

WARWICK
I know *that*.

SANDY
You do?

WARWICK
Corse. I'm having a beer with Peter on Thursdee. Said
he can't remember her exactly but he employs over a

hundred people at the track. So I'm showing him a photo on me mobile-

SANDY
(exacerbated)
Not Peter Thompson! PeTA!! People for the Ethical Treatment of Animals. She's at the track *protesting*. Not laying on trifectas!

WARWICK
You're bloody kidding me!

GRAHAM
(aside)
Lolita never said anything about this. Although she was cagy when I asked about her bloodlines.

Warwick tears off stage-left.

GRAHAM (cont'd)
(to band)
Is this what they call leaving Act#1 on a dramatic arc? Boys, if you will indulge me.

Graham turns to the band and conducts a suspenseful chord.

END ACT ONE

ACT II

SCENE 1

INT. FELICITY BLISS'S FLAT GOSFORD - DAY

Tabatha and Felicity sit drinking tea.

TABATHA
Well, Darling, it would never have worked. You *rescue* dogs. Warren *kills* dogs.

FELICITY
Warwick. For the upteenth time his name is Warwick, Mother. You know that. And he doesn't kill dogs. He races dogs.

TABATHA
Okay, whatever it is those people do up here for leisure in God's Waiting Room.

FELICITY
Do you know how he trains his greyhound?

TABATHA
A feral cat tied to a stake?

FELICITY
With a squeaky toy, down the beach.

TABATHA
Really?

FELICITY
(flatly)
Yeah, it's a huge conspiracy. Tea?

TABATHA
I'll just have a-

FELICITY
I know. I know. A cup of hot water.

TABATHA
Make it a mug, darling.

Felicity exits.

FELICITY (O.S.)
How's the detoxing going?

TABATHA
Wonderful, Darling. Wonderful.

Tabatha takes out a coffee plunger from her handbag.

Felicity returns with a mug of hot water.

TABATHA (cont'd)
Oh and some milk.

FELICITY
Milk?

TABATHA
Milk and hot water. All the rage in the Himalayas.

Felicity exits.

TABATHA (cont'd)
Bruno wants to add you to WasteBook, or whatever you
Millennials call social media, these days.

FELICITY (O.S.)
Mum, I'm not interested in men like Bruno. I liked
Warwick. He was sweet. And just happy to be himself.

And I felt I could be myself around him. It was
something different.

Felicity returns.

TABATHA
Forget Warren. Bruno has a villa in Naples, Darling.
And guess what? It's not built from fibro.

FELICITY
Fibro? What is it with you and fibro?

TABATHA
Whenever I come up here to visit you Darling in
Boganville, all I see is fibro, fibro fibro.

FELICITY
I like to call it 'Central Coast Tudor'.

TABATHA
(thinking)
You know, I think death is a lot like Gosford.

FELICITY
Why?

TABATHA
It's easy to get to but not a lot happens when you get
there.

FELICITY
It's that horrid motel you stay in at Wamberal? Why not
camp here overnight?

TABATHA

What, and sleep on a milk crate? No thanks Darling.
Besides they do a fabulous mojtio there and the beach is
only three-hundred elbow-crawls from my room.

FELICITY
Why not simply drive back to Sydney?

TABATHA
It's too *tiring* coming up and going back to Paddington
in one day.

FELICITY
People commute to Sydney for work everyday from the
Central Coast.

TABATHA
(thinking)
I know, bless. I'm sorry, Darling. Yes it's lovely up here;
with the pretty beaches and everything. But you sit on a
beach and look around and behind you and it's nothing
but Boganville.

FELICITY
Really??

Tabatha sings and dances her heart out.
"BOGANVILLE"

UNDER A TROPICAL BREEZE
YOU JUST PLEASE YOURSELF SWEATING
BUT AREN'T YOU FORGETTING
YOU ARE IN BOGANVILLE

UNDER A TROPICAL SUN
YOU DRINK FIVE MARGARITAS
WHILE THOSE DRUNKEN SIGNORETAS

TAKE A LEAK IN THE POOL

I SAY THIS TWO-STAR MOTEL
IS FROM HELL
AND I'LL LEAVE
OH MANANA
AND I'M SHOCKED
WHEN MY TOILET IS BLOCKED
AND THE GARDEN'S LANTANA
AND MY CAB'S A TORANA
WHEN YOU'RE IN BOGANVILLE

AND SO YOU STROLL TO THE BEACH
JUST TO SNATCH A SIESTA
BUT THE LOCALS DO PESTER
WHEN YOU'RE IN BOGANVILLE

AND THE NIGHTLIFE IS DEAD
SO YOU HEAD FOR THE ONE RSL
BUT THE FOOD IS FROM HELL
WHEN YOU'RE IN BOGANVILLE

THE DECOR YOU IGNORE
BUT THE BINGO NEXT DOOR
DRIVES YOU LOCO
AND THE VEAL IN YOUR MEAL IS NOT REAL
BUT THE CHEF'S ON A SMOKO
AND YOUR PEAR
IS A CHOKO
WHEN YOU'RE IN BOGANVILLE

(INSTRUMENTAL BREAK)

THE EVENING RUSTLE OF PALM FRONDS
SUCH A ROMANTIC SETTING

BUT AREN'T YOU FORGETTING?
YOU ARE IN BOGANVILLE

UNDER THE LIGHT OF THE MOON
YOU'RE CONSOLED BY MOJITOS
IN YOUR ROBE OF MOSQUITOS
YES YOUR SOLE IS FINITO
WHEN YOU'RE IN BOGANVILLE

TRANSITION TO:

EXT. WAMBERAL BEACH - DAY

We hear a seascape as Lorry and Warwick walk
Graham along the beach. Graham sits down and pulls
out the form guide from the Tele.

LORRY
(looking up)
Beautiful day. No rain for days, they reckon.

WARWICK
(looking up)
You know what that means.

LORRY/WARWICK
(nodding)
"Slugs"

Warwick throws an imaginary ball on a stick over the
audience. Graham drops his paper and lethargically
strolls after it.

LORRY

Geeze, he's not in great form today, is he?

WARWICK
He's not the same dog, Dad. Not since the
announcement of the ban. And since he's not playing
with Lolita anymore, he's really down in the dumps.

LORRY
Mate, if you don't mind me saying, you're not the same
bloke anymore, either. Not since-

WARWICK
Flick? Felicity?

LORRY
Mate, I can see you looking for her out the corner of yer
eye ever since we got here.

WARWICK
(chuckles sadly)
Yeah I spose I am.

LORRY
(pointing out into the audience)
Son, see that ocean out there?

WARWICK
Yeah?

LORRY
There's plentya fish in it.

WARWICK
Yeah, but this fish was kinda special, Dad.

LORRY

Was she a fish or a mermaid?

WARWICK
Mermaid?

LORRY
Well...as you know, your grandad was a professional
fisherman. He used to reckon some shelias were
mermaids. You know? Wrong-uns. Bad omens.

WARWICK
That's right. For old sailors and fishermen mermaids
were associated with storms and shipwrecks and
drownings, right?

LORRY
Yep. The old man reckoned some blokes were scorpions
and some women were mermaids.

WARWICK
Yeah, I kinda remember Pop talking about it once when
we were out in the tinnie.

LORRY
He reckoned some blokes ended up chasing mermaids
all their lives. Bouncing from one bad relationship to
another.

WARWICK
Yeah?

LORRY
Anyway, mate, I've gotta get going. Got a load of apples
in the truck. Got to get it up to Maitland Woolies this
arv. See yer tonight for tea.

Lorry exits.

Warwick frisbees and imaginary pebble into the ocean and sings.

WARWICK
(sings)
"MERMAIDS"

I SEE YOU IN THE OCEAN
I SEE YOU IN THE CLOUDS
I HEAR YOUR VOICE IN SEABIRDS
I LOOK FOR YOU IN CROWDS
I FEEL YOUR WARMTH IN HARBOURS
BUT THEN THE VISION FADES
OH HERE I GO AGAIN I'M CHASING MERMAIDS

I FIND YOUR SOUL IN ISLANDS
I HEAR YOUR VOICE IN RAIN
I FEEL YOUR STRENGTH IN OCEANS
AND WITH THE TIDE YOUR BACK AGAIN
I FIND YOUR SMILE IN SUNLIGHT
BUT THEN THE VISION FADES
OH HERE I GO AGAIN I'M CHASING MERMAIDS

SINCE YOU LEFT ME WAITING
I WANDER BY THE SHORE
I SCAN EACH LONG HORIZON
AND WANDER ROUND IN STORMS
TO HOLD YOU IN MY ARMS AGAIN ONCE MORE
IS ALL I LONG FOR
OH HERE I GO AGAIN I'M CHASING MERMAIDS

(INSTRUMENTAL BREAK)

SINCE YOU LEFT ME WAITING
I WANDER BY THE SHORE
I SCAN EACH LONG HORIZON
AND WANDER ROUND IN STORMS
TO HOLD YOU IN MY ARMS AGAIN ONCE MORE
IS ALL I LONG FOR
TO FOLD YOU N MY HEART AGAIN ONCE MORE
IS ALL I LONG FOR
OH HERE I GO AGAIN I'M CHASING MERMAIDS

TRANSITION TO:

EXT. GOSFORD SHOWGROUND RACE TRACK - NIGHT

Lorry, Showbags and Beer Bottle are at the track, beers and form guide in hand.

SHOWBAGS
Mate, if you don't mind me saying, Graham is having a shocker tonight. What's the story?

LORRY
It's this ban, Bags. He's lost the mongrel in 'im somehow. You throw a ball down the beach he lights up a smoke before chasing after it. He's not the same dog.

Lionel enters the stage with an angry Tyson on a leash/muzzle.

LIONEL

Harrigan, that dog of yours is utterly *useless*. He ran like a sack of shit, tonight.

LORRY
Lionel, he's just not himself these days.

LIONEL
I'd get the mongrel back in 'im. At me private track. menacingly A special discount for a Harrigan.

Lionel and Tyson exit.

BEER BOTTLE
He's right. Bags and I have been talking about it, Loz. You might have to consider a night with the devil.

LORRY
That idiot? Surely you're not serious.

BEER BOTTLE
Mate, if you want to place at Sandown before it's all over in NSW, you're gunner have to get the mongrel back in the dog. Lionel's yer only hope.

Graham (muzzle) - panting, buckled over and out of breath - is led to the stage by Gary.

GRAHAM
(panting and buckled over)
Sorry boys. Tyson wrong footed me at the turn.

GARY
Graham, you were chasing the pack all the way, mate. Dad, I've got to check some dog piss. I'll catch you all later.

LORRY
No worries.(to the boys) ...Dr Harrigan!

Gary exits.

GRAHAM
Sorry Lorry. I'm just not feeling it, like I used to.

BEER BOTTLE
Mate, we think you might need a day with 'he who shall
not be named'.

GRAHAM
Not that fucken Lionel?

Showbags and Beer Bottle nod.

GRAHAM (cont'd)
What and chase some poor bloody feral cat around a
track that he's got tied to a stake. I've heard the other
dogs talking. What's wrong with Warwick's squeaky
toy? I love the squeaky toy.

SHOWBAGS
Mate, we've got to get the mongrel back in you, if you
want to place at Sandown and finish on a career high.
You're not gunner win races drinking schooners and
reading the Tele all day. That's gotta stop, right now.

GRAHAM
(patting his belly)
Yeah, I have let meself go a bit. We all have. It's only
Lionel's boys that are still chasing hard. And I reckon
most of em are suffering from Post Traumatic Stress
Syndrome.

LORRY
Yeah?

GRAHAM
I've seen it before. Look at Tyson. You disembowel a
possum, it stays with you.

BEER BOTTLE
Mate, I could eat a possum and chips, right now.
Lemme tell ya.

LORRY
Yeah, how's the new diet going, mate?

SHOWBAGS
You on a diet, Bottle?

BEER BOTTLE
Yeah, it's for me Tinder profile.

Shows the boys (and audience) a pic of him in sluggos.

LORRY
Mate, you're not fat.

BEER BOTTLE
According to me BMI - body mass index - I'm obese.

SHOWBAGS
Mate, the BMI is a con. I always use the FCI. It's more
of an Australian standard.

LORRY
What's the FCI?

SHOWBAGS

The Fishing Club Index. I stand next to the blokes at the bar in me fishing club and I'm positively anorexic.

BEER BOTTLE
Anyway, Bags and I reckon were "too poor to be thin".

LORRY
Too *poor* to be thin? How do you work that out?

BEER BOTTLE
Well, you go to a deli and buy a healthy lunch you don't get any change from $15.

SHOWBAGS
Yeah, I still got a smoked-salmon salad on lay-by.

BEER BOTTLE
Where as you can buy a Cheeseburger from Maccas for two bucks. You do the math.

SHOWBAGS
Loz, we're just too *poor* to be thin.

LORRY
Whaydda mean?

BEER BOTTLE
Well, since it's a musical. Let us explain through the highly emotive medium of song?

LORRY
(indicating the audience)
Mate, don't tell them that. You're breaking the third wall. (thinking) Or is it the glass ceiling.

SHOWBAGS

It's the forth dimension.

GRAHAM
It's the fourth *wall*.

LORRY
What?

GRAHAM
The fourth wall is a theatrical term for the imaginary
"wall" that exists between actors on stage and the
audience. Showbags...Beer Bottle...over to you.

SHOWBAGS/BEER BOTTLE
(sing their heart out)

"I'M TOO POOR TO BE THIN"

WE'D BE EATIN' SUSHI
ALL DAY LONG
INTO HEALTHY LIVIN'
BUT FINDIN' THE MONEY HONEY
(ALL) WE'RE TOO POOR TO BE THIN

WE'D BE EATIN' SALMON
ALL NIGHT LONG
TUNA WE'D BE STEAMIN
BUT FINDIN' THE BREAD
TO LOSE OUR SPREAD
(ALL) WE'RE TOO POOR TO BE THIN

I CAN SEE YA THINKIN THAT WE'RE TOO FAT
LOSE SOME WEIGHT BEFORE IT KILLS YA
I CAN SEE YA LOOKIN'
AT OUR BEHINDS

BUT WE WILL
(ALL) RIOT ON A DIET

WE'D BE PUMPIN' IRON
ALL WEEK LONG
BABY WE'D BE SWEATIN'
BUT FINDIN' A GYM TO LET US IN
(ALL) WE'RE TOO POOR TO BE THIN

(INSTRUMENTAL BREAK)

I CAN SEE YA THINKIN THAT WE'RE TOO FAT
LOSE SOME WEIGHT BEFORE IT KILLS YA
I CAN SEE YA LOOKIN'
AT OUR BEHINDS
BUT WE WILL
(ALL) RIOT ON A DIET

WE'D BE PUMPIN' IRON
ALL WEEK LONG
BABY WE'D BE SWEATIN'
BUT FINDIN A GYM TO LET US IN
(ALL) WE'RE TOO POOR TO BE THIN
(ALL) WE'RE TOO POOR TO BE THIN
(ALL) WE'RE TOO POOR TO BE THIN

TRANSITION TO:

EXT. WAMBERAL BEACH - DAY

Felicity is walking along the beach with Lolita.

LOLITA
You know this is the first time you've taken me here
since you met him here last time.

FELICITY
Really?

LOLITA
Yes.

FELICITY
I liked him a lot. I don't know why. On paper it
shouldn't make sense. But when he held me I felt
something I've not felt before with anyone else. I can't
quite explain it.

LOLITA
They say opposites attract. I shouldn't like Graham
either. He's a jock. I'm into books and music.

FELICITY
Crazy, isn't it.

LOLITA
Yep. They say we're enamoured of that which eludes us
the most. Anyway, I'm off to sniff some turds. I'll leave
you with your thoughts.

FELICITY
(sings)
"HOLD ME"

HOLD ME
NEVER WALK AWAY
AND SCOLD ME
TAKE ME IN YOUR ARMS

AND FOLD ME
INTO YOUR HEART
AND WHEN YOU TOLD ME
NOT TO BE AFRAID
BUT TO TRUST IN YOUR HEART
THERE'S NO NEED TO BE SO
SCARED OF THE DARK
WHEN THE LIGHT I NEED
IS YOU

NEED ME
DON'T ENDEAVOUR TO MISLEAD ME
OPEN ALL THE DOORS
THAT LEAD ME
STRAIGHT TO YOUR HEART
AND TAKE ME
INTO YOUR SECRET PLACE
AT THE FOOT OF YOUR SOUL
BY YOUR SACRED GRACE
I WAS HALF NOW I'M WHOLE
WHEN I STUMBLED INTO YOU

HOLD ME
IN YOUR TENDER ARMS
AND MOULD ME
WITH YOUR MYSTIC CHARMS
AND FOLD ME INTO
A CORNER OF YOUR HEART

TRANSITION TO:

INT. RADIO STUDIO - DAY

The stage is dark and we see a giant slide of Jesus wearing a set of recording headphones.

In the darkness we hear conversation in voice over.

HALLSY (V.O.)
On the line we have Lorry from Gosford. Let's hear how King Baird is driving people to move interstate with the imminent shut-down of the dog racing industry. Let's examine how Chairman Baird's decree, his *outrageous* lone wolf decision affects the Little Battler. So let's hear from the Voice of the Voiceless. The man in Struggle Street. Good morning, Lorry. My producer tells me you're looking to move to the Gold Coast, is that right?

LORRY (V.O.)
Um...hello? Is that you, Hallsy?

HALLSY (V.O.)
Yes go ahead, Lorry. You're on air. This decision mate. You must feel like killing yourself.

LORRY (V.O.)
No not killing myself but yes I was looking at a move to the Gold Coast but Sandy - that's me misuss - reckons it's too hot and full of white-shoe property developers.

HALLSY (V.O.)
Well, there's nothing wrong with property developers. And they don't all wear white-shoes. Indeed, we have one who sponsors this very program.

LORRY (V.O.)
Well, that's were you let yourself down Hallsy. You gotta remain neutral in life, champion. Property

development is what this is all about. My mate Beer
Bottle reckons...

HALLSY (V.O.)
Beer Bottle?

LORRY (V.O.)
Yeah, we call him that cause there's nuthun from the
neck up. You know, he's not right in the head. Likes
bangin' grannies.

We hear dial tone.

LORRY (V.O.) (cont'd)
Hellooo...hellooo...Hallsy...?

TRANSITION TO:

EXT. GOSFORD SHOWGROUND RACE TRACK -
NIGHT

Lorry is ticking off numbers on the form guide. A
steward holds Graham on a leash/muzzle in the stirring
pen. Lorry chats over the waist-high fence.

LORRY
How do you think you'd go against Barnacle Bill,
tonight mate?

GRAHAM
Oh you mean Freddie? Yeah, I think I could take him if
I have the inside box. I've been sledging him in the
boxes, lately. Works a treat. "You've got no balls." "Is
that a tick in your ear?" "Gee heart worm is bad at the
moment." That type of thing. Really gets under his fur.

LORRY
I don't go in for sledging as a rule. Winning isn't
everything. But we *do* need some kinda edge at the
moment, mate. You're running like a fat man to a diet
centre.

GRAHAM
(indicating other dogs)
Shhh! They'll hear you. Hey, isn't that your brother over
there? No, doubt about the bloke. He's always on the
blower making some sorter deal. Anyway, I'm off. It's
Jane's first race and she's so nervous she's spewed
everywhere.

LORRY
Poor thing. You off to comfort her?

GRAHAM
Are you kidding? I'm off to lick up her spew.

LORRY
Yuk.

GRAHAM
What can I tell you? These are the ways of my people.

Graham exits singing a line from Billy Joel's *NY State of
Mind* "...I'm taking a Greyhound down the Hudson
River line...".

Charlie enters, speaking into his phone.

CHARLIE
(into phone)
Mate, I've just spotted my little brother. I'll have to call
you back. Yep yep. Just hold off on that decision till I

consult my partners. I need to do some due diligence, first.

Charlie hangs up.

LORRY
Hello, Charlie! Mate, so good to see you. You in town *again*? You've got to let us know so when you're down on the Coast so we can have you over for dinner. The boys would love it. Sandy has a marinated feral pig shoulder in the freezer. Her brother Andy shot it. So it's fresh as. Sandy marinates it in red wine. Bewdyful. Hey, what does "Due Diligence" mean? I heard you say on the phone before.

CHARLIE
It means doing your homework.

LORRY
Fancy words. That's a university education, for ya.

CHARLIE
(flattered)
You don't need an economics degree to know what due diligence means, Loz.

LORRY
You always were the brains of the outfit, Charlie. Wish I was more like *you*.

CHARLIE
Lozy, let me ask you a question. If I had a dog that needed a little... how can I put it?...extra zip in his step, who would be the man to see on the quiet at Gosford?

LORRY

I didn't know you had a dog, Charlie?

CHARLIE
I keep hearing the name Lionel...?

LORRY
Mate, I don't go in for that sorter thing as a rule, as you know. Most of us don't do that. Just a few rotten apples-

CHARLIE
Yeah yeah I know that Loz. But the biggest rotten apple would be...?

LORRY
Lionel. Yeah, Bags and Bottle - mates of mine - reckon Graham - that's me dog over there licking up spew - needs to visit Live-Baiting Lionel but hey, winning isn't everything, right?

CHARLIE
Wrong! Don't you want to go out with a bang? Give your dog the winning edge?

LORRY
Sure. Sure. Be great to go out on a high. But you gotta remember, it's blokes like Lionel that have *wrecked* our sport.

CHARLIE
But winners are grinners, Lorry.

LORRY
You know, life's not all about winning, Charlie. Don't you remember the old man telling us that? We'd be out fishing in the tinnie and you'd always have to catch the

biggest fish. Or the most fish. The Old Man would always say, Charlie-

CHARLIE
That's where you're wrong, little brother. It's *all* about winning. Getting the edge on your competitor. That's why I drive a Ferrari and you drive a twenty-year-old Commodore. Look at Alan Bond and his winged keel and the Americas Cup?

LORRY
Wasn't Alan Bond a crook and a bankrupt?

Graham returns and listens.

CHARLIE
You're missing the point, Lorry. Look at your history. Look at Nelson at Trafalgar. Wellington at Waterloo. Life belongs to the winners! The victors! The conquerors!

Graham salutes.

LORRY
The Old Man used to say: Life is about the people who are in it.

CHARLIE
Do you want your dog to win or not, Lorry?

LORRY
Yes, but like I say, wining isn't everything.

CHARLIE
You're right.

LORRY
Really?

CHARLIE
(sings, Graham dances)

"WINNING ISN'T EVERYTHING IT'S THE ONLY
THING"

WINNING ISN'T EVERYTHING IT'S THE ONLY
THING
LOSING AFTER A BRUISING
IS SUCH A LONELY THING
NOW IF YOU OWN A DOG
SPARE ME THE MONOLOGUE
YOU ONLY THINK OF VICTORY
NEVER CONTEMPLATE DEFEAT
LOSING'S CONTRADICTORY
NEVER SOUND THE OLD RETREAT
CAUSE WINNERS ARE THE GRINNERS
LOSERS ARE THE SORE
CAUSE WINNING ISN'T EVERYTHING IT'S
MORE!

WINNING ISN'T EVERYTHING IT'S ALL WE
KNOW
ALMOST IS SUCH A SMALL BOAST
SUCH A FEEBLE CROW
NO SELF-RESPECTING MALE
EVERY SOUGHT TO FAIL
CAUSE WINNING MADE AUSTRALIA GREAT
CAUSE WINNING'S ALL WE'VE GOT
WE'VE NO ROOM FOR FAILURES MATE
SO GIVE IT ONE LAST SHOT
CAUSE WINNING IS THE GREATEST

LOSING'S FOR THE FOOLS
WINNING ISN'T EVERYTHING IT RULES!

NOW THINK OF NELSON
AGAINST THE SPANISH AND FRENCHIE FLEET
HE WENT THROUGH HELL SON
TO SEE 'EM SINKING
AND SEE EM BEAT

NOW THINK OF PATTON
WHEN YOUR FLAT AND
STARING AT DEFEAT
BUT WHEN ALL ELSE FAILS
TO TIP THE SCALES
YOU SIMPLY HAVE TO
CHEAT!
(LORRY) CHEAT?
CHEAT.

WINNING ISN'T EVERYTHING IT IS THAT AND
MORE
YOU NEVER ADMIT YOU'RE A LOSER
UNTIL THE FINAL SCORE
WHAT SCARLET-BLOODED MAN
BECAME AN ALSO-RAN?
UNTIL YOU'VE HEARD THE WHISTLE BLOW
THE FATTEST LADY SING
LAUNCH YOURSELF LIKE A MISSILE THROW
YOUR HAT INTO THE RING
CAUSE WINNING IS FOR CHAMPIONS
LOSING SURE DOES STING
CAUSE WINNING ISN'T EVERYTHING IT'S KING

(INSTRUMENTAL BREAK)

NOW THINK OF MANLY OR
SCOTT AMUNDSEN ANTARCTICA
OR THINK OF STANLEY
WHO GOT AMONGST EM
IN AFRICA
NOW TAKE PEARL HARBOUR
AND THE YANKEES
LOSING HALF THEIR FLEET
OLD YAMAMOTO
WHEN HE SANK HE
SIMPLY HAD TO CHEAT!
(LORRY) CHEAT?
CHEAT.

WINNING ISN'T EVERYTHING IT'S JUST WHO
WE ARE
IT'S THE SILVERWARE, THE GOLDEN RING
THE BIG CIGAR!
MEN WHO SHARE A DREAM
WILL THINK OF ANY SCHEME
CAUSE THERE'S NO ROOM FOR HEDGING BETS
YOU RACE THIS DOG TO WIN
NOW'S THE TIME FOR SLEDGING LET'S
GET RIGHT BENEATH THEIR SKIN
CAUSE WINNING IS FOR WINNERS
LOSING'S FOR THE SORE
WINNING ISN'T EVERYTHING IT'S MORE

TRANSITION TO:

INT. HARRIGAN FAMILY HOME GOSFORD -
NIGHT

Sandy is grooming Graham. Lorry walks in and throws his bag down in disgust.

LORRY
The world has officially ended.

SANDY
Why?

LORRY
First the dog racing ban. Now the gearbox in the truck has packed it in for good. I've got a load of bananas in the back headed for Singleton. I'll have to get Showbags to take it up in his truck for me. (looks up to heavens) What have I done to offend you?

SANDY
How much will a new gearbox cost?

LORRY
More than we've got in the bank.

SANDY
We've got zero in the bank.

LORRY
We'll think of that number and add twenty grand.

SANDY
Lorry this is a *disaster*.

LORRY
I'm gunner have to ask him.

SANDY
Over my dead body.

LORRY
Luv, we've got no choice. He's me brother.

SANDY
Don't you see? This is *exactly* what he wants.

LORRY
(exacerbated)
He wants me to have no truck. No income. Lose the
house? You're being hysterical.

SANDY
(furious)
Hysterical? Don't you patronise me, Lorry Harrigan.

LORRY
(chuckling to himself)
You've never got over the fact that he dumped you.

SANDY
(apoplectic)
Dumped me? I keep telling you. I dumped *him* for you.
And he's *never* got over it.

LORRY
What *are* you smoking? The bloke's dating twenty-year-
olds with fake tits. I don't think he's crying into his beer,
Sandy.

SANDY
Is dating twenty-year-olds with plastic tits your measure
of success?

LORRY
Corse not. I'm just saying, if he's carrying a torch for
you, he's hiding it rather well.

SANDY
Well, you can go and get fucked, Lorry Harrigan! Yer
dinner's in the oven. I'm off to the club. And if I win the
jackpot on the pokes, I'm buying a convertible and
leaving you. And don't be here when I get back!

Sandy exits.

GRAHAM
She doesn't mean that.

LORRY
I know that.

GRAHAM
She'd at least take me with her.

Lorry paces and thinks.

LORRY
If I just could get you back on bunny we could win that
big one at Sandown. Pay off everything. Debt free. But
you're running like a pensioner to a bingo hall.

Lorry whips out his mobile.

GRAHAM
Who are you texting? Sandy.

LORRY
My brother, Charlie. I'm taking you to see Lionel,
tomorrow night.

GRAHAM
Have you completely lost your *mind*?

LORRY
We've got no choice, mate. Charlie says its the only way
to get the winning edge. And he'd know. Just don't tell
Sandy. I don't know who she hates more. Sandy or
Lionel

TRANSITION TO:

INT. FELICITY BLISS'S FLAT GOSFORD - DAY

Felicity is at home reading a book *The Girl With The
Dogs* by Anna Funder. Her mobile rings.

Lotita is reading Mikhail Bulgakov's *The Heart of a
Dog*.

FELICITY
(into phone)
Yes, this is the Central Coast office of peTA - well not
officially - the phone's diverted to me while Terry's on
the Rainbow Warrior this month. How can I help? Live
baiting in Gosford? (jumps to her feet) Tomorrow?
Hang on I'll write down the address. (writing) okay. Got
it. I'll alert the media. What time is it taking place? Got
it. Who? Lionel Dunstan and Lorry Harrigan? And
what's *your* name?

Felicity is open-mouthed.

FELICITY (cont'd)
Charlie Harrigan A.O.?

Felicity hangs up. Lolita puts down her book.

LOLITA

Harrigan?

FELICITY
Says he's Lorry's brother. But I don't understand. After that terrible dinner, I talked to Warwick about it and he said his family never went in for that.

LOLITA
What are you going to do?

FELICITY
I haven't worked it out yet.

TRANSITION TO:

INT. HARRIGAN FAMILY HOME GOSFORD - DAY

Sandy is grooming a labradoodle. Gary is checking it.

Warwick reads a newspaper.

SANDY
(feeling the dog)
Does that feel right, Gary. Feel this lump?

GARY
(feeling the dog)
Yeah, it could be just a cyst. We'd really need to do a biopsy to be sure.

SANDY
I agree. I'll tell the owner. She keeps saying she'll take it to the vet but never gets around to it. That's why I called you over from work. While I have the dog here.

A doorbell rings.

SANDY (cont'd)
That'll be the owner now.

Gary exits.

Felicity enters.

Gary enters behind her, trying to make calls on his mobile.

SANDY (cont'd)
(to Gary)
What does *she* want?

WARWICK
What are *you* doing here, Flick?

GARY
She has some news you need to hear.

SANDY
We're all being locked up for owning a greyhound?

WARWICK
Carn Mum! Give her a go.

FELICITY
I've come to tell you, your husband's being set up by this own brother.

SANDY
Charlie?

GARY

Charlie's called the offices of PeTA to say Dad and
Lionel are blooding Graham tonight.

SANDY
The stupid idiot. This is all about bloody Sandown. He's
obsessed with that race. Thinks it'll solve all his
problems. One big win...

WARWICK
Can't believe Uncle Charlie would do this to us?

SANDY
I can. That brother of his is so crooked, if he'd swallow
a nail, he'd shit a corkscrew.

FELICITY
Where *is* Lorry?

WARWICK
Mum and him had a big fight. He's sleeping on Beer
Bottle's couch.

FELICITY
He's sleeping on a couch made from beer bottles?

WARWICK
Long story.

GARY
I've tried calling but Dad won't answer his phone.

SANDY
It's probably dead. He forgets to charge it if I don't
remind him.

WARWICK

What will we do, Mum?

SANDY
We better get around to Bottle's house now. See if we can nip this in the bud before he gets in any deeper. (soto voce) Dickhead. He'll never forgive himself.

GARY
I'll grab my keys.

SANDY
(to Felicity)
You must be *loving* this.

GARY
Mum, give her a break. She didn't have to come round here to tell us anything.

SANDY
Tell me. Does my dog look like he's being mistreated?

FELICITY
This isn't about you personally, Sandy. It's about the mistreatment of dogs everywhere. The mistreatment of animals, generally.

SANDY
I suppose they're being mistreated when they come to me for a shampoo and blow dry.

WARWICK
Mum, dogs are mistreated all over the world. In Bali they are sold for food. In China they have a huge festival and eat them. Felicity's emailed me pictures. It's heartbreaking. It's makes *Four Corners* look like *Playschool*.

GARY

He's right Mum. I see cruelty to animals all the time as a
vet. There was a time when homo sapiens where just
another animal fighting for survival on the savannah.
But we've evolved to be the cruelest of animals. But not
all of us. (to Felicity) Not everyone in the dog racing
industry is live baiting and killing dud dogs. Just like
not everyone in PeTa is blowing up labs and sending
death threats to scientists. Most of us all want a better
deal for animals.

SANDY

Let's get to Bottle's joint, now. Carn, get yer skates on.

GARY

I better drive. You're too upset, Mum.

Gary and Sandy grab some keys and leave.

Felicity and Warwick, alone, face each other.

WARWICK

Are you going tonight? With the film crew? Film Dad's
public shaming?

FELICITY

Yes. I'm afraid I am. We've heard about this Lionel for
years. We're worried that with all the tabloid hysteria,
people have forgotten what this was all about in the first
place.

WARWICK

Well, I appreciate you tipping us off. Mum will too.
Eventually. When she calms down. Dad's not himself
lately.

FELICITY
Well, I also thought it was an excuse to see you. We
never did get a chance to say goodbye, properly.

WARWICK
(chuckles)
Yeah I guess you and I are about as different as people
could be.

FELICITY
(chuckles)
I'd say so.

WARWICK
I'll see you when I see you, I guess.

FELICITY
Yeah, see you when I see you.

"SEE YOU WHEN I SEE YOU"

GOODBYE

TRANSITION TO:

EXT. LIONEL'S SECRET RACE TRACK - NIGHT

The stage is dark. Off-stage we hear people singing
Happy Birthday in the distance.

Lorry and Graham enter gingerly, holding flashlights.

Their flashlights reveal auxiliary cast members in cages in various animal suits. Here the cast improvise: "is this a hotel? Did you know anything about the possum in cage two? His name was Douglas. There's a bad smell in here" etc etc.

The caged cast members shush each other when Lionel enters.

Tyson follows.

Lights up.

The stage is transformed into a macabre circus ring. Lionel is wearing crazy clown makeup (al a Heath Ledger as The Joker) and holds a butcher's knife aloft.

LIONEL
(ringmaster like)
Welcome to the wheel of death!

LORRY
That's a bit dramatic, isn't it Lionel.

LIONEL
(flatly)
Did you bring the cash?

LORRY
Yes but-

LIONEL
(dramatically)
Tyson, bring on the first contestant!

Tyson exits, only to return with "Tabatha" in a raggedy cat suit tied to a stake like Joan of Arc. The "cat" is terrified.

GRAHAM
Loz, you know I hate cats. But I can't do this. Look at her paws. This old gal's been living on the street for years. Mate, this isn't me. This isn't you. This isn't the Harrigans. Look she's absolutely shitting herself. And not in a good way.

LIONEL
Don't worry, Lorry. I've seen this before. Leave it to me.

Lionel puts down the knife and pulls out a treat from a packet of Smackos. It's a Smacko tied to a string.

He sways it in front of Graham's eyes.

Graham is mesmerized.

GRAHAM
No no no! Not the Smacko. I'll do anything for a Smacko. Everyone knows that.

LIONEL
Look into my eyes, Graham. You know you want this Smacko. You would do anything for this Smacko. You would *kill* for this Smacko.

GRAHAM
(hypnotised)
Yes. Yes. It's true. I would kill for a Smacko.

LORRY
Lionel, I'm uneasy about this.

139

Lorry repeatedly clicks his fingers in front of Graham.

LORRY (cont'd)
Graham. Graham! Snap out of it. I've got Smackos in the car.

GRAHAM
(coming around)
It's true. Lorry, its true.

LORRY
What's true?

GRAHAM
Dogs go wacko for Smackos.

TYSON
(singing manically in tremolo)
Dogs go wacko. Dogs go wacko. Dogs go wacko for Smackos.

LIONEL
Tyson! That's enough! Lorry this is your last and *only* chance to win the Super Dog Series. I'm popping back to the house for a beer and will let you think it over. I can't be here all night, waiting. We have people over tonight.

LORRY
In that makeup?

LIONEL
It's my granddaughter's birthday. We couldn't afford a clown.

GRAHAM

(recoiling)
Jesus!

LIONEL
You've got fifteen minutes. Once she blows out the candles. I'll be back to start the wheel of death!

TYSON
(chants)
The wheel of death! The wheel of death!

LIONEL
Tyson, the knife. I need it to cut the cake.

Tyson grabs the knife. Lionel and Tyson exit.

GRAHAM
Is it just me or is that guy totally bonkers?

LORRY
Sorry Graham. I don't know what I was thinking. I'm just not meself these days. This is awful. Let's get outta here.

We soon hear *For She's a Jolly Good Fellow*.

LORRY (cont'd)
Quickly. Before he comes back!

GRAHAM
You know...I'm not really a cat person but...

Graham unties the cat from the stake.

The cat menacingly puts out her claws to Graham. Graham pulls out $20.

GRAHAM (cont'd)
Woo woo there kitty. Here's take this. Get yourself a hot meal. And lady, you really need a shower, dude.

The cat dramatically sings a line or two from "Memory" from Lloyd Webber's *Cats*.

The orchestra suddenly all yell "kill her! Kill her, now."

The cat snatches the cash from Graham and bolts from the stage.

GRAHAM (cont'd)
(to audience)
Remember, pets aren't just for Christmas. She probably came from a good home, once.

Lorry and Graham exit.

Lionel and Tyson return wearing paper hats and eating birthday cake.

We hear sirens.

Police lights flicker at the corner of the stage.

Lionel and Tyson are open-mouthed.

LIONEL
Tyson, we've been rumbled! Open the cages!!

TRANSITION TO:

EXT. WAMBERAL BEACH - DAY

Lorry and Warwick enter. Warwick holds a ball on a stick. They stare into the distance.

WARWICK
Beautiful morning, Dad. No rain for days, they reckon.

LORRY
(looking up, squinting)
  You know what that means?

WARWICK/LORRY
Slugs.

Lorry nods, gravely.

Lorry looks into the distance.

LORRY
(chuckling)
  Geeze, Graham loves the beach, doesn't he?

WARWICK
It's his favourite thing.

LORRY
That, and Smackos.

WARWICK
Graham! Leave that dead fish! (to Lorry) You know, I can't believe Uncle Charlie could do that to his own brother.

LORRY
Yeah, seems Charlie was looking to develop the showground into townhouses. He's got some big players

in his pocket, too. Some people think that's what this whole ban is about.

WARWICK
Dad, I've heard that conspiracy theory but I've come to realise the ban's about people like Lionel.

LORRY
(nodding, resigned)
Yeah, it's about people like Lionel.

WARWICK
I hear he's facing a prison term.

LORRY
His granddaughter will be upset.

WARWICK
I still can't believe Uncle Charlie sold you out like that. Why would he do it? He's rich. He doesn't need the money.

LORRY
Did Pop ever tell you about the frog and the scorpion?

WARWICK
No.

LORRY
The Old Man told it to me when we were out fishing one day.

A scorpion asks a frog to carry it across a river. The frog hesitates, afraid of being stung, but the scorpion argues that if it did so, they would both drown. Considering this, the frog agrees, but midway across the river the scorpion stings the frog, dooming them both. When the frog asks the scorpion why did you sting me? Now we will both drown. The scorpion replies:"it's in my nature".

WARWICK
(nodding)
I think I understand.

LORRY
In life, some women are mermaids. Some blokes are scorpions.

WARWICK
Speaking of women, how are things with you and Mum?

LORRY
Well, I'm still sleeping on Beer Bottle's sofa, if that answers yer question. Geeze that bloke could snore for Australia. Fair dinkum.

Graham excitedly enters the stage, dropping a dead bird at their feet.

GRAHAM
(panting)
I just saw Lolita and Felicity up the other end of the beach. They're headed our way!

WARWICK
So?

GRAHAM
So?? *So*??? This is your chance, Woz. To get back with her, I mean.

WARWICK
It's all over between us.

GRAHAM
Aren't you forgetting something?

LORRY
What?

GRAHAM
This is a musical. It needs a happy ending.

LORRY
(indicating the audience)
You can't tell them that. You're breaking the fourth
ceiling.

GRAHAM
(exacerbated)
For fuck's sake! It's the "fourth wall". What's *wrong*
with you people.

WARWICK
Fourth wall, is it?

GRAHAM
Well, if you don't try. I certainly will. I love that dog.
I'm going to do the most romantic thing a dog can do.

LORRY
What's that?

GRAHAM
I'm going to lay a huge turd at her feet and sing my
heart out.

Lolita trots on stage.

GRAHAM (cont'd)
Lolita, Lolita. I just want to say...I mean I'm...if only...I
wanna...it's just...

LOLITA
Dog, can't you speak?

GRAHAM
(shrugs)
Nabokov once said 'I think like a genius, write like an
author, and speak like a child.'

LOLITA
(smiling)
You *have* been reading your Russians.

GRAHAM
All for you, Darling. All for you. But I have something
here for you that words can't express.

LOLITA
(rolling her eyes)
Oh really.

GRAHAM
Wait till you see *this*!

Graham crouches, looking behind himself and nods
impressively.

GRAHAM (cont'd)
(pointing)
Tell me that's not the *best* turd you've ever seen on
Wamberal Beach!

LOLITA
(looking down her nose)
  Turds don't impress me.

GRAHAM
Are you *kidding* me? You can't fool *me*. No dog can
resist a hot steaming turd!

Graham sings his heart out.

Lolita joins him on the final fecal-happy chorus.
"TURDS"
(TO BE WRITTEN)

EXT. GOSFORD SHOWGROUND RACE TRACK -
NIGHT

Lorry, Showbags, and Beer Bottle are at the track
sucking on beers and studying the form guide.

BEER BOTTLE
Geeze, did you hear about, Lionel?

LORRY
What's the latest?

BEER BOTTLE
Isn't *he* in the shit.

SHOWBAGS
Hey, isn't that your misuss over there?

BEER BOTTLE
Look out she's heading over. Crash helmets on
everyone.

LORRY
Just give us a few minutes, boys, will ya?

Showbags and Beer Bottle exit.

Sandy enters.

LORRY (cont'd)
What are *you* doing here, Sandy?

SANDY
(sighs)
They reckon this is the final race at Gosford before the
ban takes place. Thought we should say goodbye to the
old place together. Thanks for the flowers, by the way.

LORRY
It was nothing.

SANDY
I know it was. Next time take the card out of them that
reads *Frank, we will always miss you.* Tell me you
didn't pinch them from the side of the road.

LORRY
(pleadingly)
I'm *broke*!

SANDY
(sighs)
Well, it's the thought that counts, I spose.

LORRY
(sighs)
You were right about, Charlie.

SANDY
So was my old man.

LORRY
Your old man? God, didn't he hate me.

SANDY
Hate *you*? Not true.

LORRY
(sniggers)
  Yeah right.

SANDY
Old Dad never said much. But when I was seeing you
and Charlie and I couldn't decide, he once said: one
brother will bring you great wealth. One brother will
bring you great love. You choose.

LORRY
(shocked)
  Did yer old man really say that?

SANDY
Yep.

LORRY
Does this mean I can come back home and give you
more great love?

SANDY
Yep.

LORRY
Good. Cause one more night on Bottle's couch and I'll
never walk again.

They both laugh.

Warwick, Gary, Showbags and Beer Bottle rush onto the stage, excitedly.

WARWICK
Dad, dad, have you heard the news?

SANDY
What news?

GARY
The Premier's just held a press conference. He's over-turned the dog racing ban! We've won, Dad! The fight's over. We've bloody won!!

They all cheer.

LORRY
(indicating the track)
So all this won't become townhouses?

GARY
No. We are here to stay, Dad!

GRAHAM
(wide-eyed and open-mouthed)
This means my career's back on track!

WARWICK
You bet it does!

GRAHAM
(open-mouthed)
It's dream come true!

LORRY
It's a dream come true for all of us!

GRAHAM
This is the happy ending to the musical we've been
waiting all for, Lorry. Oh, crap, I better head off. I'm in
the next race. Now Tyson's banned, I reckon I'm a
chance. And Loz, because I'm out of form, the bookies
have me at a hundred to one. You want that new
gearbox? Put a hundred smackers on the nose. And I
don't mean Smackos!

SHOWBAGS
Good on ya, Graham!

GRAHAM
Shh! Don't call me that now. My stage name's Kinky
Boots, rememebr? I've got to get into in character.
(exiting) I'm *back* baby! I'm *back*!

Graham exits. We hear him off-stage shouting, "I'm
back, I'm back. You hear me?"

We hear a text 'ding'. Warwick looks at his phone.

LORRY
Who's that? Charlie?? He'd be hating this.

SANDY
I can see why he texted and didn't call.

LORRY
Why's that?

SANDY

Cause his voice is three octaves higher since I went over to his hotel last night and kicked him square in the balls.

LORRY
Ouch!

WARWICK
(reading)
No, it's Felicity, actually.

Warwick chuckles to himself.

LORRY
What does she say?

WARWICK
(reading)
She says *you must be happy with the reprieve. Now there's only one thing left to do.*

LORRY
What's that?

WARWICK
(reading)
Earn it.

GARY
(nodding)
How true.

We suddenly hear the announcer call the race.

The cast turn to the audience and start cheering on Graham.

Graham wins.

LORRY
You little bewdy! Here he comes now. Go collect him
Warwick.

Warwick exits.

SHOWBAGS
Graham *bolted* in. What a race!

BEER BOTTLE
Never seen nuthun like it me life! Told ya to stick with
him, Bags.

LORRY
Here he comes. The little champion!

Warwick returns with a **real greyhound** on a leash.

LORRY (cont'd)
(patting dog)
Here he is! Well done mate. Well done. I've got a whole
packet of Smackos for yer.

SHOWBAGS
Graham, you won by a country mile!

BEER BOTTLE
We've cleaned out the bookies!

LORRY
I know. I know!

BEER BOTTLE
You know what this means but.

LORRY
Yep. I'll be racing him at Sandown. I'm movin' up to the city, boys.

SHOWBAGS
Sandown? Nah. Think bigger.

LORRY
Bigger than Sandown?

BEER BOTTLE/SHOWBAGS
Las *Vegas*!

LORRY
(sings)
"MOVIN' UP TO THE CITY"

I'M SITTIN' HERE IN'A GOSFORD PARK
PICKIN' ALL THE PUPPIES JUST AS SOON AS IT'S
DARK
SICK'A PICKIN' PUPPIES FOR NO REAL REASON
HOPE I'M NOT HERE PICKIN' FOR ANOTHER
DAMN SEASON
GUESS I'M KILLIN' TIME
WITH NOTHIN' TO LOSE
PICKIN' ALL THE PUPPIES AND A SUCKIN' ON
BOOZE

I DON'T DIG THIS TRACK ONE BIT
HAD ENOUGH OF THIS COUNTRY SHIT!
I'M MOVIN UP TO THE CITY
(ENSEMBLE) HE'S MOVIN UP TO THE CITY

I'M SICK AND TIRED OF RUSTIC CHARM
SICK'A THE COUNTRY, SICK OF THE FARM

THE CITY'S MIGHT PRETTY WHILE YOUR
CHEWIN ON CUD
OR BREAKIN YOUR BUTT WITH A MUTT IN THE
MUD
SICK'A KILLIN TIME
FOREVER IT SEEMS
TIME TO DIP MY CUP INTO A BUCKET OF
DREAMS

I DON'T DIG THIS TRACK ONE BIT
HAD ENOUGH OF THIS COUNTRY SHIT!
I'M MOVIN UP TO THE CITY
(ENSEMBLE) HE'S MOVIN UP TO THE CITY

INSTRUMENTAL BREAK AS THE CAST DANCE
THEIR HEARTS OUT.

I'M SICK AND TIRED OF RUSTIC CHARM
SICK'A THE COUNTRY, SICK OF THE FARM
THE CITY'S MIGHT PRETTY WHILE YOUR
CHEWIN ON CUD
OR BREAKIN YOUR BUTT WITH A MUTT IN THE
MUD
SICK'A KILLIN TIME
FOREVER IT SEEMS
TIME TO DIP MY CUP INTO A BUCKET OF
DREAMS

I DON'T DIG THIS TRACK ONE BIT
HAD ENOUGH OF THIS COUNTRY SHIT!
I'M MOVIN UP TO THE CITY
(ENSEMBLE) HE'S MOVIN UP TO THE CITY

Lorry and the cast sing and dance their dog-lovin' hearts
out...

Felicity and Lolita enter dressed as Las Vegas show-girls.

Charlie enters dressed as Elvis in a white jump-suit.

Showbags dances with Tabatha.

Beer-bottle is dancing with a granny plucked from the audience and waving a tiny French flag.

Graham (actor) enters as himself.

It's big, it's brash, it's the finale to a smash hit musical!

THE LIGHTS FADE TO BLACK...

The cast return to take their bows to an instrumental reprise of 'Turds'.

<u>THE END</u>

OTHER TITLES AVAILABLE FROM
ORiGiN™ THEATRICAL

MILLIE'S WAR
Dorian Mode

Based on historical events, Millie's War is set in the 1980s, when a number of women attempted to join official ANZAC Day marches across Canberra to commemorate women raped in war. Fourteen women were arrested. The following year, again in Canberra, around 250 women attempted to join the tail of the official ANZAC Day march but were stopped by police. The police were acting under a Section 23A of the Traffic Ordinace, a section conveniently gazetted the day before the march.

Approximately 64 people, mainly women, were arrested and charged.

With this dramatic backdrop, Millie's War is set largely in the boardroom of an RSL Club. When the sleepy local branch of this RSL meet with the women in order to dissuade them from upsetting their sacred parade of remembrance, the crotchety president of the RSL Club is appalled to find his own granddaughter is one of the feminists attempting to spoil their day. Tempers soon reach boiling point as each side argues the case for the importance of commemorating victims of war.

Casting: 4M, 3F
Full Length Play, Australian, Comedy, 1910s / WWI, 1980s

www.origintheatrical.com.au